Macramé for Adult Beginners

The Comprehensive Guide For Learning Macramé With Ultimate Knots & Techniques And Creative Projects With Step-by-Step Instructions

By

Alexia Ann Barlow

Disclaimer

Contents

Introduction

The fascinating weaving technique known as macramé uses knots to create a wide range of textiles. Recently, the macramé art form has become more popular. Crafters and artisans are coming up with inventive ways to use macramé outside of the typical wall hangings and plant hangers. The popularity of this ancient ritual has fluctuated over thousands of years. However, this system will remain in some capacity because of its usefulness.

Yes, macramé has changed over time as a result of the continual, multifaceted creative process. Both novice and seasoned macramé makers will discover the craft to be calming, enjoyable, fulfilling, and creative. For those who simply want to utilize and adore the final products, there are an increasing variety of excellent macramé options to match your home, attire, and personal taste.

Currently, the ability and enthusiasm of macramé mean various things to various individuals; for some, it is priceless and unique in several ways, whereas for others, it is irrelevant.

Your hands and arms will get stronger using the knot-tying technique known as macramé. Making a macramé item can be a creative way to go green while also being very peaceful and delightful for the mind, body, and spirit. These are just a few of the advantages that fans of macramé claim the art form offers its practitioners.

Macramé provides benefits beyond the countless beautiful and useful things it produces. In its most basic form, macramé is therapeutic. The arms and hands are strengthened by pulling and using ropes.

It helps keep joints lubricated. Some individuals consider the contemplative art form of macramé, which uses repeated knots to create designs, to be soothing. All a hobbyist needs to get started exploring macramé's endless possibilities is some twine and some basic knots. There are only a few supplies and equipment needed to make macramé.

To bring macramé into the globe of contemporary living, Macramé for Beginners combines the age-old craft of creative knot-making with intriguing new design ideas. We have put together a wide range of tempting projects to suit all your creative aspirations, whether you are searching for an aesthetic feature to liven up a space or decorative yet utilitarian elements to alter your entire home.

We have something for everyone, whether you want to pick up a new skill or simply develop an existing one. There are numerous projects to select from. Our designs use a variety of rope thicknesses, vibrant color schemes, and intriguing textural approaches to introduce you to a wide range of creative options.

There is a comprehensive guide to knot tying, and we strongly suggest that you practice the knots you will use before starting a project. If you allow yourself enough time and take things slowly, surely you will succeed.

Chapter 1: What is Macramé?

The art of macramé involves knotting cords to create decorative and useful products. You can create something by just knotting the cord if you have any. Instead of using weaving or knitting techniques, macramé uses knots to make textiles. Sailors have historically decorated their ships and other items with macramé, which is also used to produce wall hangings, bags, mats, jewelry, and plant hangers.

In macramé, a variety of knots and knot combinations are utilized, such as the square knot, half a knot, lark head knot, and coil knot. Numerous different designs can be created depending on the knots used and whether they are used alone or in conjunction with others.

For macramé, a variety of natural and synthetic cords in a wide range of hues, textures, and sorts are available. Practically anything you can tie into a knot will work, and you can find the necessary supplies in a variety of stores, including craft, hardware, DIY, needlework, and sewing shops.

Although some materials are frequently used in various projects, this does not indicate that others will not work just as well. In some circumstances, the material used will be determined by what is being constructed, but in others, it may be feasible to experiment with your selections.

This method's simplicity and convenience of use contributed to the global spread of macramé, even before it had its beginnings in ancient Egypt and the Incan empire. It has a lengthy history in Japan as well; braided vine cords and bracelets from the Jomon era ruins site at Sannai Maruyama, Aomori, have been discovered, and the macramé trend has been around ever since.

There was a significant craft craze, particularly during the Showa era (1926–1989), when individuals made lampshades out of knitting spools, bags out of knotted silk threads, and other items.

The popularity of macramé, which was at the time popular in the West as well, increased in Japan in 1978 as a result of the founding of the Japan Macramé Popularization Society. It has recently experienced a comeback in the form of bags, accessories, hanging plant holders, and more. And the list keeps expanding, with macramé playing a more and bigger part in high-end fashion and textile art.

1.1 Brief History of Macramé

It is thought that Arab weavers in the thirteenth century were the ones who invented macramé. By tying the knots out of the extra thread & yarn that was left over along the edges of hand-loomed materials like bath shawls, towels, & veils, these talented artisans produced decorative fringes.

The Arabic phrase "migramah," which is considered to mean "ornamental fringe," "stripey towel," or "embroidered veil," is where the word "macramé" originates. This term is derived from the Spanish word "macramé."

The art was first taken to Spain after the Moorish conquest, then it was moved to Italy, notably to the Ligurian region, and eventually, it was spread throughout Europe. The English people were first shown it at the palace of Mary II in the late seventeenth century. Queen Mary was reputed to teach her ladies-in-waiting how to make macramé.

During their downtime at sea, sailors would make macramé items, which they would then sell or trade once they reached port, thereby introducing the craft to other locations like the New World and China.

Macramé was used by sailors from the United Kingdom and the United States during the nineteenth century to create bell fringes, hammocks, and belts. They referred to the method as "square knotting," just after the knot that they utilized the majority of the time. Sailors also named macramé "McNamara's Lace."

During the Victorian era, macramé was at the height of its popularity. A popular book published in 1882 called Sylvia's Book of Macramé Lace instructed readers on how to "For colored and black outfits, sew elaborate embellishments, both for garden parties, home wear, seashore wandering, and balls— adornments for the home and linens with a fairy-like aesthetic."

This craft was used to decorate the majority of Victorian dwellings. Macramé was utilized in the production of utensils and furnishings for the home, such as bedspreads, tablecloths, and curtains.

Macramé was once all the rage, but it fell out of favor for a while. In the 1970s, however, it became fashionable again as a technique for making wall hangings, articles of clothing, bedspreads, little jean shorts, draperies, tablecloths, plant hangers, and other home decor items. By the beginning of the 1980s, the fad of using macramé as a decorating technique had already started to go out of style.

Macramé, on the other hand, is experiencing a resurgence in popularity. This time, however, in the shape of jewelry, specifically bracelets, necklaces, and anklets of various kinds. This type of jewelry is characterized by its primary use of square knots and its frequent use of handmade glass beads & natural components like gemstones, bone, or shells.

Cords composed of cotton thread, linen, hemp, leather, jute, or yarn are only some of the materials that can be used in macramé. Knots, as well as a wide variety of beads (made of stone, glass, or wood), pendants, and shells, are typically used in the process of creating jewelry. Sometimes, rings or gemstones are used as focal points for necklaces. These focal points might be wire-wrapped to enable the necklace to be fastened, or they can be encircled in a web-like array of interweaving overhand knots.

1.2 What is Macramé Produced of?

Materials that can be utilized for macramé include cotton twine, nylon, linen, yarn, jute, leather, and hemp. Choosing the best material for your project is determined by the following qualities:

Strength: The cord's strength depends greatly on how it was made, specifically whether the individual threads were braided or twisted. Hemp, leather, jute, and nylon are some of the most durable.

Texture: Particularly if you create macramé jewelry, you do not want harsh material on your skin. Due to its propensity to soften with wear, hemp makes a great textile. Leather and cotton are also excellent choices.

Stiffness: You should utilize flexible material that can be bent. While thicker cords are typically stiffer, thinner cords are typically more flexible. Hemp and cotton both have a smooth, flexible texture that makes them ideal for jewelry-making. Make sure to pick leather that is no wider than 2 mm if you intend to utilize it.

Diameter: The thickness of a macramé cord is listed in millimeters when you purchase one. Carefully consider the thickness, especially if you plan to add beads, buttons, or other decorations.

1.3 Materials of Macramé

For the creation of macramé goods, a cord is required. Any string-like object that can be tied can be utilized; however, for clean shapes, we advise using a cord with appropriate tension and little elasticity. In this section, we will focus on the four materials most frequently used in macramé, including cords made of cotton and hemp.

Cotton

The fundamental component of the macramé cord. Cotton cords come in both twisted and braided varieties. Start with the braided cord because it is simpler to work the knots and see them easily. Once you are more comfortable, switch to the twisted cord.

1. A fade-resistant, colorfast cord that is perfect for accessories.

2. The easy-to-knot braided cord is advised for novices.

3. On interior goods, the loose twist works well as a fringe.

4. Use it for making large items because it is thick.

5. Use thick rope for display and interior decor objects.

Hemp

There are several kinds of hemp for diverse purposes, including varieties manufactured from the jute plant and the hemp plant. Hemp typically contains fibers that stand out, unlike cotton.

1. Jute is hefty, making it ideal for large interior objects like hangings.

2. Superior hemp that will not irritate. Since the color will not fade, accessories can use it.

3. As the cord's fibers protrude, it is advised to only be used for hangings and other inside items.

4. Like parcel string in appearance, when you want to manufacture something quickly and cheaply, it is an excellent option because it is affordable.

5. Being braided makes it easier to knot, and it does not itch.

Synthetic Fibers

The fact that synthetic fibers are all lightweight and maintain their color is their most important quality.

1. Ideal for manufacturing bags because the finished product is lightweight.

2. Ideal for creating accessories, it is coated with resin, making it difficult to undo, and it can be fused to keep it in place.

3. Thick and sturdy. This cord has a fused option.

4. Resembles silk in luster. Also appealing since loops may be formed easily despite their hardness.

5. The process of melting the strands at the ends of a cord with a flame from something like a cigarette lighter prevents fraying.

Leather and Natural Materials

Natural materials are appealing because of their distinctive texture. Be careful not to get the leather wet, as it can fade.

1. Round leather cord with a shine. Four different thicknesses are available.

2. A flat cord produced from cowhide. It is nice to see it turn a toffee hue as it ages.

3. A round leather cord with a nap. It has an understated feel to it.

4. A four-strand braid of oiled flat leather. It has a presence even as it is.

5. Rope made from the strong sections of abaca fiber. Easy to work with when wet.

1.4 Different Kinds of Macramé Cord

Macramé cord is a general term for all the different kinds of fibers that can be used for macramé. This includes rope, yarn, string, and some waxed choices. They also come in various thicknesses, which will affect the result you want to get. It is up to you to decide what you want to use. Still, it would assist if you attempted to utilize the same thickness as the sequence said to. Here are a few options you have:

Rope

The rope is a material most frequently used for macramé creations. It gains additional strength and thickness via the twisting of several strands around one another. There are numerous varieties, including braided six-ply and twisted three-ply ropes. Macramé rope forms unusual, substantial knots that are difficult to untwist.

String

The numerous tiny fibers that make up a string are twisted together to form a single strand. It is hence much lighter than macramé rope.

You can tie much smaller and tighter knots using string.

Yarn

Yarn, which is frequently used for knitting or weaving, can also be utilized for macramé. It can have multiple strands twisted together and is typically constructed of wool & industrial hemp; however, this is not always the case.

Waxed Cord

For macramé jewelry, a smaller-diameter waxed string is commonly utilized. The cord can be plied or unplied; it is coated in beeswax to strengthen it and is water-resistant. There are many different hues available, though wax generally makes the tints darker.

Chapter 2: Supplies for Macramé

2.1 Options for Working Surfaces and Suspension

Project Boards

These boards are quite useful because they are frequently pre-labeled with measurements. While some are foamy and soft, others are strong and durable, while still others are self-healing.

If your project needs stability, project boards are a must. Both tape and pins typically work just as well on them. They can occasionally be constrained by scale. They are frequently most effective when used for smaller-scale projects, like jewelry making. The measures and grid keep designs consistent, especially when tying straight rows and netting.

Cardboard and Foam Core

Do you require an alternative to a project board? Cardboard and foam core could come in handy. Measurements can be inserted by hand, and they are frequently available at a moment's notice, but they are not self-healing, and they might not keep the pins very steady.

Just be careful not to pierce the rear of your board with the pins when utilizing thinner boards and foam core. There will be an "ouch!" about that. However, using pins may not always be essential.

Hooks and Lines:

What about substantial hanging projects? If working directly on the ground or a table, you have a variety of possibilities (just do not cut it):

- **S-Hooks:** These are available from your neighborhood hardware shop, garden center, or plant nursery in a range of sizes. S-hooks may be hung from a hook that is fastened to the ceiling, a rail, a door, or the back of a chair.

- **Wreath Hanger:** Wreath hangers, which are widely accessible throughout the holiday season, provide a secure hook for hanging unfinished work. This is useful for tying longer projects because it allows you to sit or stand comfortably.

- **Temporary/Roll-Away Garment Rack:** An open and stable suspension zone is provided by a garment rack when it is coupled with a few S-hooks or is just loosely linked to the bar. In the home organizing sections of the majority of big-box stores, garment racks come in all shapes and sizes.

2.2 Essential items

T-Pins

Because they are less cumbersome than thumbtacks or pushpins, T-pins are suggested as a working companion for project boards.

Scissors and Shears

For every project in this book, scissors can be used, but if you wish to use a coarse string, like jute or sisal, you might want to use gardening pruners to make the cuts to prevent damage to the blades from your preferred trimmers.

Measurement Ruler or Tape

Each project in this book begins with a certain quantity of cord. Both metric and imperial systems follow the same rules. Please pick one and use it consistently for the duration of the pattern.

Tape

This is particularly useful when applied to twisted materials. While you work, it prevents the cord from unwinding. A small amount of clear-drying glue added at the end of your finished piece helps keep the ends neat and secure.

Which kind of tape do you require? Any tape you have on hand, such as temporary hold or washi tape, should function without a problem. The stronger the tape, the better since if you end up cutting the taped portions of your work off, you could lose up to 1/4" (0.61cm).

Glue

The fact that adhesive is not required is one of the best things about needlecraft. Glue is only used to seal the ends of ropes to keep them from fraying. Fabric glues that dry clear will have the strongest grip. Common classroom glues will work just as well for projects (like wall hangings) that will not be exposed to water.

2.3 Extras

Gloves

Your hands may get tired from working on a huge rug or another labor-intensive activity. Working gloves may save your flesh if you deal with a cord that is very wiry, hairy, or coarsely textured, like jute. For a beautiful home design, there is no need to rub your skin raw!

Beads

It can be challenging to find macramé beads. The majority are constructed of wood, but if you look attentively, you can find ceramics. The only measurement for a bead that needs to be taken into consideration is the size of the threading hole.

Although they are hard to locate in jewelry stores, beads with holes between 6 and 10 mm can be found. You might need to use the Internet to find the perfect size for ceramic and stone-style beads. Remember that since metrics are the most widely used unit of measurement, beads are typically measured in this way.

Rings

Rings occur in a variety of materials, including metal and wood. Stocking up on 1 1/2" to 2 1/2" (3.81 to 6.35cm) sizes is recommended when working with plant hangers, even though they can be hard to find.

The majority of plant hanger projects may be changed so that they do not utilize rings, but they are useful and a good place to start for such projects. Embroidery hoops work as stand-ins in a pinch.

Use embroidery hoops just for simpler macramé creations because the wood is relatively light. In situations where a larger ring is required for a project, Hula Hoops are a great choice. They come in handy, especially for making wall hangings and enormous dream catchers.

Dowels and Rods

While it is easy to find wooden dowels at your neighborhood hobby, craft, and hardware store, mother nature also offers a variety of branches, twigs, and driftwood that can be utilized as project supports.

Splicing Equipment

When a knot is too complicated, splicing tools can be used to help lengthen the length of a cord. Here are a few alternatives since it can be challenging to locate these tools:

- Beading tool

- Trombone paperclip or flowery wire (formed into a hook)

- Crochet hook

Sewing Supplies

When working with fabric, a thread and needle may be more than sufficient, but occasionally a sewing machine is simply faster.

Chapter 3: Beginner Macramé Terms

Understanding patterns for projects might be incredibly complex when you are just starting. The best kind of string to purchase is completely a mystery. Here are 19 terminologies related to macramé that every novice should be aware of.

What is the sinnet? Braided as opposed to twisted? When all you desire to do is make lovely fiber art, the process can be enough to drive your head spin. What do you mean, we understand!

So let's discuss some macramé terms.

Let's start by unraveling the macramé thread mystery. There is rope, cord, and string. There are three main types of materials, and which one you pick should depend on the final appearance of your project.

Macramé String

Single-twisted, incredibly soft macramé string is typically manufactured from cotton. It is ideal for wall hangings and makes a beautiful fringe. Because you want to ensure that your plant hangers will support the plants, so don't hesitate to pair them with plant hangers. If you need to untie & retie it too frequently, be careful because it is not very tolerant to rework.

Macramé Rope

Three cotton strands are commonly knotted together to form macramé rope. Although it is less soft and more durable than string, it is the ideal material for plant hangers. The reason we like a rope over other materials is that it maintains its shape, is simpler to untie & retie, and, when fringing, has a wavy appearance that, in our opinion, is more modern bohemian.

Macramé Cord

Typically, 6 strands are braided together to make a macramé cord. It can be constructed of polypropylene or cotton (plastic). A cord is a fantastic material to use when your project requires a lot of weight support because of its strength.

Now that the secret has been cleared up, let's discuss some vocabulary that will make understanding a macramé design feel more natural.

3.1 Knots for Beginners and Their Acronyms

Lark's head knot (LHK)

Your project requires the application of a lark's head knot to secure the rope. Additionally, it can be used to join ropes together. The loop is in front. The rope is covered by the dowel rod to do this.

Reverse lark's head knot (RLHK)

Just the opposite of what was stated above. Which method you tie a lark's head knot will depend on how you desire your piece to look. Take the rope under & over the dowel rod to tie the reverse lark's head knot.

Half Square Knot (HSK)

A square knot's left side. A spiral design results from tying all HSK knots.

Right half square knot (RHSK)

The polar opposite of HSK. Your spiral design will be created by tying all RHSK.

Square knot (SK)

A complete square knot is created by joining a left half-square knot and a right half-square knot. In each piece you construct, square knots will be used. The simplest and most basic knot you can tie is this one.

Half hitch knot (HHK)

An excellent knot to use to create borders or boundaries is the half hitch. You can tie this knot either left or right. Since an HHK is nearly often built in pairs, the abbreviation DHHK is most frequently used in patterns.

It is also vital to keep in mind that an HHK can be tied either vertically or horizontally, which is why the abbreviations VHHK and HHHK may also be used. Are you now completely perplexed?

Alternating square knot (ASK)

ASKs are created by removing half of the cords from nearby knots and creating a new knot that sits below and between the original knots.

3.2 Additional Terms Related to Macramé

Sinnet

A column of identical knots is known as a sinnet.

When creating a sinnet of knots, square knots are typically the most often utilized knot.

Working Cords

All of the cords in a macramé creation are working cords.

Knotting Cords

The cords you use to tie the knots into your design are called knotting cords.

Filler cords

The cords that are wrapped in knots for your project are known as filler cords.

Row

A row of parallel, horizontal knots, made using a distinct working cord.

Finishing knot

A knot that's tied to secure the cord ends to prevent them from unwinding.

Gathering knot

Used to secure cords at the start or finish of a project by gathering them together.

You can understand a macramé pattern after you are familiar with these terminologies.

Alternate cords

The process of making a new knot by grouping together half of the cords from an existing knot and the other half from its neighboring knot.

Holding cord

The item—a ring, a dowel, or another rope—onto which ropes are fastened.

Chapter 4: Tips and Tricks for Macramé

Here are some simple pointers to help beginners and newcomers to the macramé craft avoid blunders and get started in their new endeavors. The secret to macramé is knotting, but before you start, consider these suggestions to help you while you are first learning.

Tip 1: It does not have to take ages to measure the cord. We offer a workaround if your project calls for numerous cords of the same length.

Two dowel sticks, each half the length of the cord you require, should be taped to your work surface. Now, wrap your cord once around each of the dowels according to the length you require. At once, cut through each loop.

Voila!

There, at the ideal length, are all the cords you require.

Tip 2: It can be challenging to tie a straight line of double half-hitch knots, especially if you are new to macramé.

To make this process easier, position a dowel rod where you want to start making the row of the double half hitch knots.

Tip 3: Due to its constant movement, trimming the fringe on your most recent work can be a pain in the neck.

After holding the fringe in place with tape, cut along the tape.

You now have a flawless fringe that stayed put when you cut it.

Tip 4: Still having trouble getting the fringe clipped straight?

Cut the fringe below the knot after bundling it together with a working cord.

The fringe must be pretty straight when you untie the knot. This can always be trimmed till it meets your standards.

Tip 5: Everyone makes mistakes, and occasionally doing so necessitates unraveling an entire work area. Fortunately, it is not always necessary to go on a mission.

Pull on the anchor cord to untie a line of double half-hitch knots. The whole row should be simple to loosen up.

Tip 6: Finding the proper cord length might be challenging, especially if you are coming up with your design rather than using a pre-existing template.

Happily, there is a workaround for that:

The quantity of cord required depends on the number of knots you are using.

As a general rule, cords should be measured at least four times longer than they need to be for your project.

If you are securing these cords using lark's head knots, double the length.

3.5 times the project length is sufficient for straightforward projects with straightforward knots, lots of fringes, and open space in the design.

Project length would need to be increased by 4.5 for complex projects.

Tip 7: When you are engaged in a project, the cord frequently unravels.

When dealing with a 3-ply cord, tie the cord ends in a knot or wrap them in tape to prevent this from happening.

Tip 8: You have incredibly extensive rope lengths available while working on a big project.

Keeping things organized while working is a challenge because these frequently become intertwined.

So why not make balls out of these long lines and secure them with rubber bands? Thus, the cords are kept tidy.

Pull a little amount from the balls as needed as the project progresses, and you need an extra cord to work with.

Tip 9: Do you have trouble establishing consistent distances between the knot patterns?

Apply a spacer! In this case, you might cut a piece of cardboard to the required size or use a dowel or ruler.

You may now design your macramé masterpiece with designs that are precisely spaced apart.

Tip 10: Fringes on finished projects frequently behave like beach hair: they fly around and make a mess.

Brush and steam the fringe before applying fabric stiffener or hair sprays to stop this from happening.

You now have a flawless fringe that will always stay in place.

There you have it, then! We hope these pointers and tactics will be useful to you as you learn to tie knots.

Additional Tips

- The hemp cord makes a good learning tool for fundamental knots because it is simple to work with and undo.

- Use nylon cording rather than silk for your early jewelry pieces once you have mastered the fundamental macramé knots. Correcting incorrect knotting is significantly simpler.

- It only functions with nylon cording when you singe the ends.

- Create a straightforward project board to serve as your workspace. It is simple to construct and portable, making your project incredibly transportable. It might be a corkboard, padded clipboard, or even a sheet of polyurethane foam, but it needs to be thick enough that pins will not slip through.

- Before you begin, make sure the rope you intend to be using fits through bead holes.

- Make a knot at the ends of the cord to prevent fraying.

- The ends of the cords can also be protected from fraying by painting transparent nail polish on them; this stiffens the ends and makes it simpler to thread those small seed beads. To accomplish the same task, you can also employ a "no-fray" liquid that is sold at fabric stores.

- Keep extra cording on hand to learn new knots.

- Consistent knotting is the secret to giving your piece a professional appearance. Perfect practice makes perfect!

- Use corsage pins instead of t pins if you do not have any on hand to attach your work. To prevent puncturing the leather cording, form an x with 2 pins to hold the cord in place. To hold the cord in place, insert pins on either side of the cord crossing in the shape of an X.

Chapter 5: Macramé Knots Guide

Items made with macramé look beautiful, but they are often too hard and complicated to make. You won't believe it, but most macramé pieces are made by putting together a few basic knots differently. There aren't many. Once you know how to tie these knots, you can use them to make any project you want.

Macramé is made up of many knots. In this chapter, we will show you how to tie all of the most prevalent knots used in macramé.

5.1 Macramé Knots

Square Knot

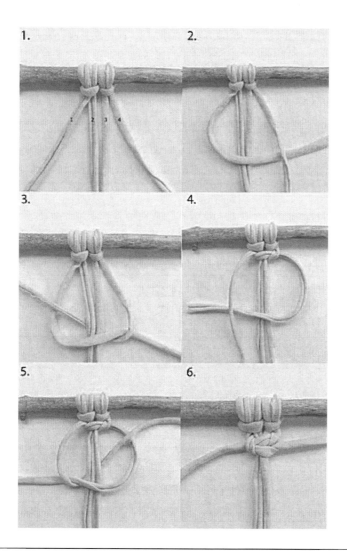

One of the most popular knots in macramé, square knots are sturdy. Two steps are needed to tie a square knot. Begin by bending the left working cord, then cross it under the right working cord and over the filler cords. Pull the right working cord through the loop the left working cord made by passing it behind the filler cords. Pull both cords slowly. We have completed half of the knot.

By doing the same action backward, you complete the knot. After bending the right working cord, cross it under the left working cord and over the filler cords. Pull the left working cord through the loop it has formed by passing it behind the filler cords. Once more, tug on both cords. You have finished!

Net Weave with Square Knots

For bags or larger pieces, the square knot can also be utilized to weave a net.

Place square knots in a single row.

After that, start knotting the subsequent row using alternate sections of rope, leaving some space between each knot.

Till your netting is the right size, repeat the same processes.

Half-Knot (HK)

The half-knot is a square knot split in half. It needs either the second half of a square knot or an additional half-knot to bind it because it is semi-unstable on its own.

Draw one working strand behind the other working strand and across the center.

After drawing the second working strand through the loop, the first working strand is created and behind the core, tighten the knot.

Overhand Knot (OK)

A widely used and straightforward knot that can be used to complete knots or to build a net using a different design. Use the same method to bind any quantity of strands simultaneously.

Create a loop at the strand's end.

Tighten the end after passing them through the loop.

Spiral Knot

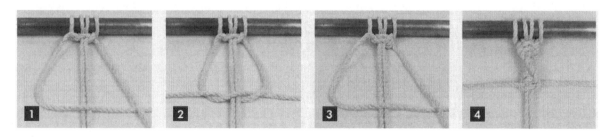

The spiral knot produces a stunning DNA spiral or helix. It works particularly well when making plant hangers.

A square knot is what the spiral knot is made of. As the knot shifts, a spiral that twists downward is created.

Begin by bending the left side working cord, then cross it under the right working cord and over the filler cords. Pull the right working cord through the loop the left working cord made by passing it behind the filler cords. Pull both cords slowly. Repeat the aforementioned steps until the spiral reaches the right length.

Wrap Knot

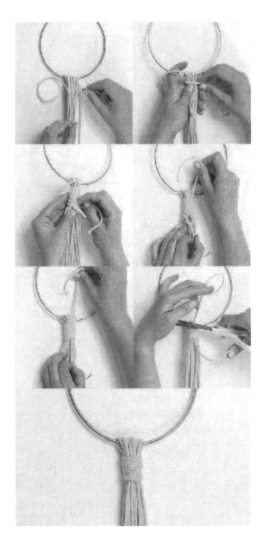

At the start or conclusion of a macramé piece, groupings of cords are fastened together using a wrap knot.

A substantial cord length was measured and cut.

In your left hand, collect the cords you want to connect. Make a downward-facing loop with the length of the cord, keeping a short tail & the remaining length of the cord at the top right.

Using your left thumb & index finger, pinch the loop's top and tail. Take the length of cable to the left and behind the group, wrap it once back around the front, then repeat the process.

Make sure the loop is still apparent at the bottom when wrapping. After tightly encircling the group, pass the remaining cord through the bottom of the loop.

Pull out the short tail end over the top of the wraps carefully to tighten the wrap knot. By catching the length and shortening the loop, the wrapped cords will be pulled upward as a result.

To make the wrap look neater, trim the tail and length at the top & bottom. Completed wrapping macramé knot.

Josephine Knot

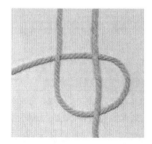 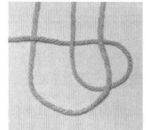 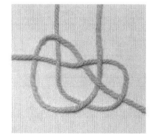 

The Josephine Knot is a beautiful knot that looks good in long, lacy styles with many strands. This knot looks very different and unique.

Create a loop with the strands on the left.

Position the right strands onto this loop, and then slip down the right strands behind the loose ends of the left strands.

Slide the ends of the strand onto the top left strands & weave the strand across the loop diagonally.

Evenly pull the knot tighter.

This knot also looks beautiful when made with more than one string.

Lark's Head Knot

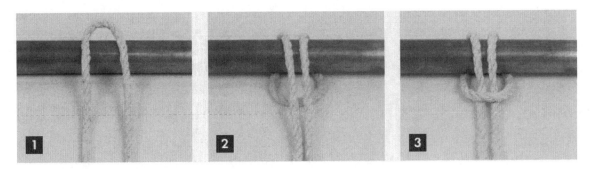

Any macramé creation should start with lark's head knots. Here's how to accomplish both front-facing and reverse-facing.

After being tied, front-facing lark's head knots leave a length of rope that rests against your dowel.

For your craft, cut and measure the length of the cord.

Fold the string in half and join the two ends.

Taking the folded loop over the dowel's top and down behind it while keeping it facing downward, start at the front.

The cord's two cut ends should be pushed through the loop and tightened to form a knot.

The vast Seed-Truth, which has blossomed and grown in so many unusual shapes, seems to have been Hermes' life's labor more than creating a school of ideology that would rule the world's intellect.

Reverse Lark's Head Knot

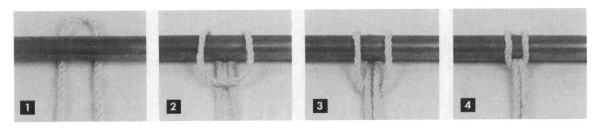

This knot is the most frequently used to fasten a length of rope to a handle or base rod.

Fold your string or rope in half, then make a loop around your handle or rod using the rope's midpoint, and then tighten the loop by inserting the tail ends.

Pay attention to how the knot changes depending on which way you thread your loop through.

Switch Knot (SWK)

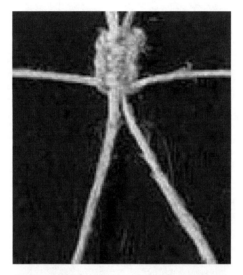

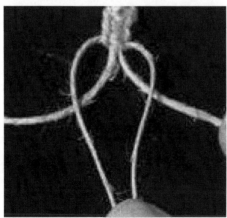

These are only a few misleading square knots, nothing more. Using a square knot to encircle the two-strand core. After tying this knot, draw the two core strands out to serve as the working strands and sandwich the working strands between them. Together with the fresh working strands, tie a square knot.

Crown Knot (CK)

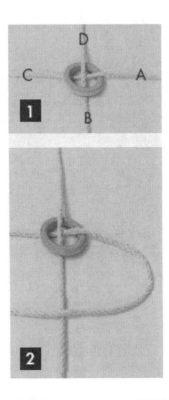

This knot appears more difficult than it is. It can be created on its own or around a core, and it needs four strands.

Start by folding the north strand over the east strand with the strands arranged out north, east, south, and west.

The north and south strands will be folded over by the east strand.

The east and west strands will be folded over by the south strand.

The west strand will fold through the north strand's loop and across the south strand.

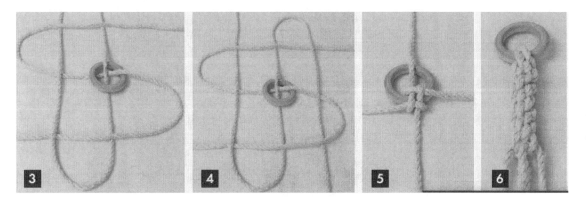

Firmly grasp the four ends. As needed, repeat the procedure.

Half-Knot Sinnet (HKS)

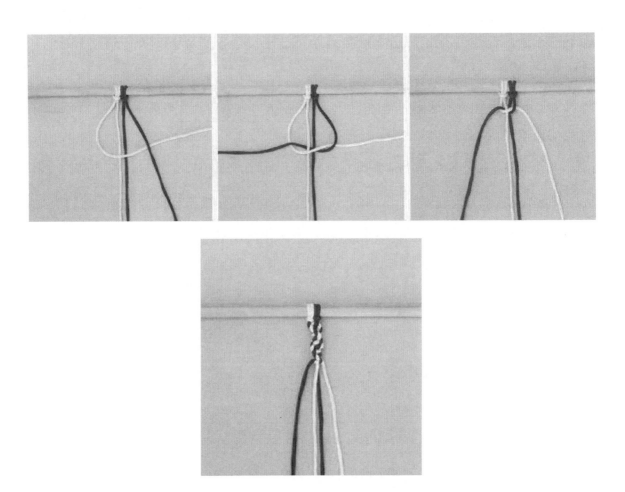

A spiral will develop if you tie a half-knot exactly more than twice. Drawing the right working strand over the core will make the spiral face left (HKLF) while drawing the left working strand over the core will make it face right (HKRF).

Gathering Knot

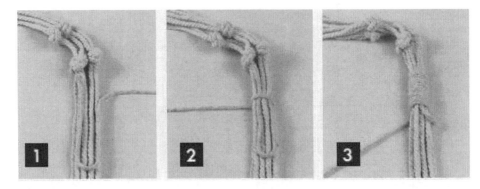

A finishing knot for gathering cords is a gathering knot, sometimes referred to as a wrapping knot. Frequently, these are located at the base of macramé plant hangers. Two functioning cords and several filler cords make up this knot.

With a different piece of cord, create a lengthy u-shaped loop with the loop facing downward on top of the collection of filler cables (this will be your working cord).

Starting beneath the top end that is pointing up, wrap your working cable around the filler cords and the loop. Make sure to reveal just a little bit of the loop.

Put the end of the wrapping cord through the loop at the bottom of your wraps.

Bring the loop under the wraps by pulling up on the end of the working cable that is protruding from the top. Till the loop is enclosed, pull it through the wraps.

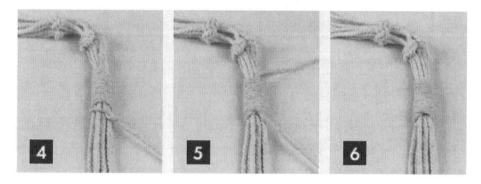

Make your gathering knot now! If you want a tidy finish, you can trim the functioning cable ends on both ends.

Half Hitch

The most adaptable knot in macramé is the half hitch. With this knot, the possibilities are endless. We'll go over the most prevalent ones: The Horizontal Half Hitch, the Half Hitch, and the Double Half Hitch.

A macramé wall hanging can be made with wavy designs by using the half hitch knot. It is the simplest macramé knot there is.

The working cord wraps around the filler cord after passing in front of it. It should be passed through the working cord's loop.

Double Half Hitch

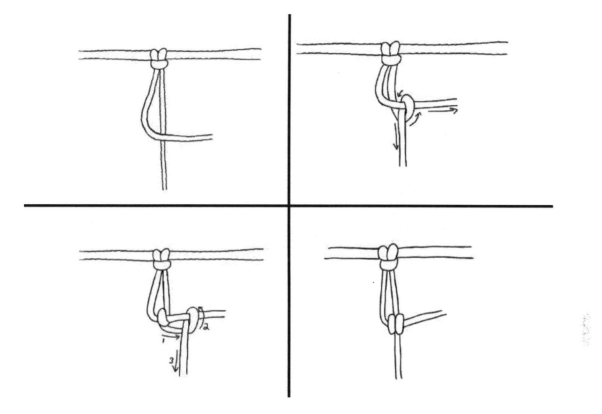

The knot that can take your creation to the next level is the double half hitch. In macramé, it is used to make various constructions and shapes.

The knot may be tied in any direction—horizontally, vertically, diagonally, or freeform. We will be examining the half-hitch knot positioned diagonally. As a filler cord, use one cord. You can use a cord or a fresh rope as your filler cord, depending on your project. The filler cord should be held at the desired angle. Pass at the back of the filler cord with your first operating cord, then loop around. To tie a double half-hitch knot, make a second loop around your filler cord.

Horizontal Double Half Hitch

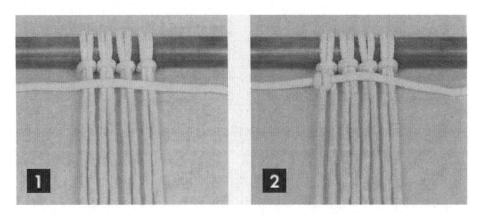

The horizontal double half hitch knot is an excellent way to add additional colors to a piece of work or to simulate a row of horizontal knots strung together. These are frequently incorporated into macramé wall hangings.

Cut a piece of the colored cord after measuring it.

Take two static cords, and then wrap them in two half-hitch macramé knots using the colored cord.

Contrary to the diagonal double half hitch knot, you must always decide which vertical static cords to tie the subsequent follow-on knots to when tying horizontal double half hitches.

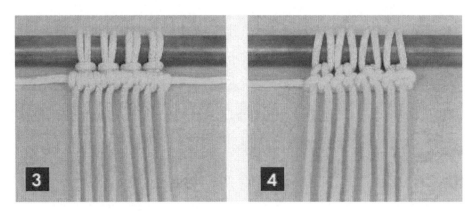

Cut the remaining cords' ends.

Double Diagonal Hitch

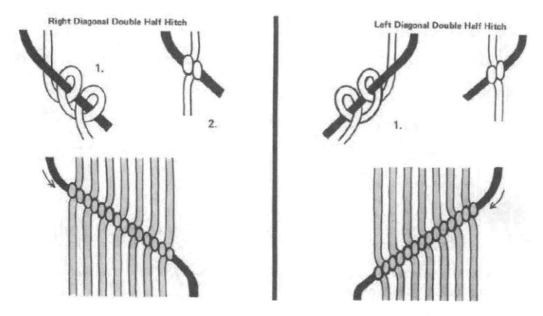

A tight flat weave produced by the diagonal half-hitch knot is appropriate for making straps and other substantial tightly woven items.

Start knitting from the right using the second cord from the right, now loop it around the initial cord, and tighten it to produce a weave that slopes down to the left. When you get to the last chord, you can start working on the following row. Next, take the third cord from the right & loop it around the second cord.

Simply reverse the steps and start knitting from the left if you want a weave that leans to the right.

Experiment around with the patterns; you can combine them into a single strap in alternate directions.

Vertical Hitch

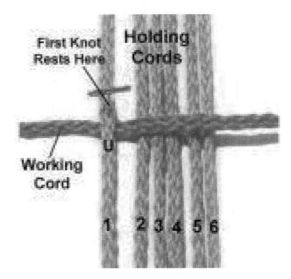

This style of hitch creates dense work that is frequently used to make carpets, wall decor, and numerous decorations, as well as belts and other accessories.

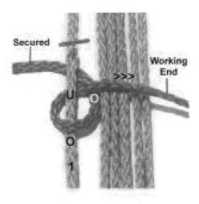

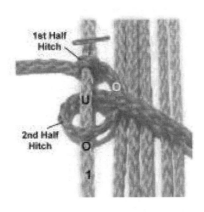

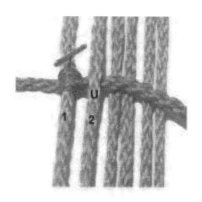

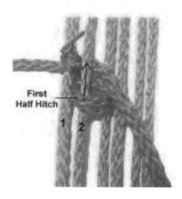

Vertical patterns are used to arrange the base threads. Double half-hitches should be made on each base thread beginning with the furthest left chord (it is going to be our working thread, and it must be at least 6 times longer than the base threads). The working thread should always be positioned above the base thread. Continue making double half-hitches from left to right. After that, move in the other direction, from left to right, and so forth.

Clove Hitch (CH)

This is a good beginning and ending hitch for fringe formation.

To knot, bring the working strand behind the anchor, loop it over the anchor front to back, and tighten it to one side.

 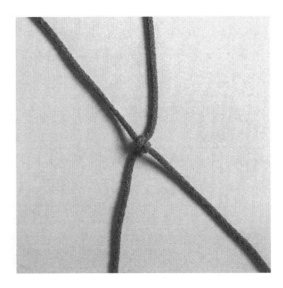

Loop over the anchor from the opposite side of the hanging strand by drawing the working strand back to the front.

After that, thread the end through the opening in the center, starting from the anchor's back, and tighten.

Diagonal Clove Hitch (DCH)

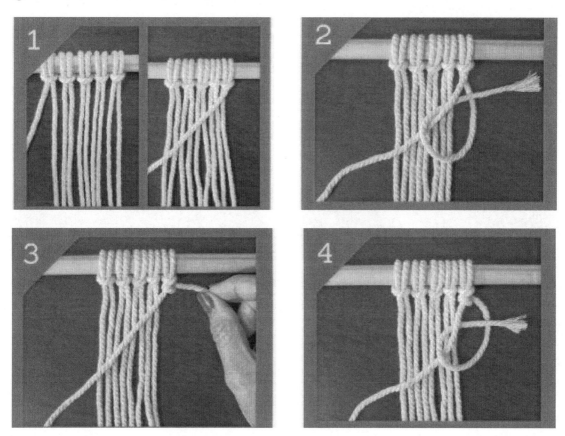

Similar to a clove hitch, this hitch can be formed in the same way. The diagonal clove hitch can be made with the anchor drawn diagonally left to right (DCHRF) or diagonally right to left (DCHLF), facing either right or left.

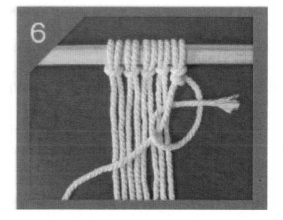

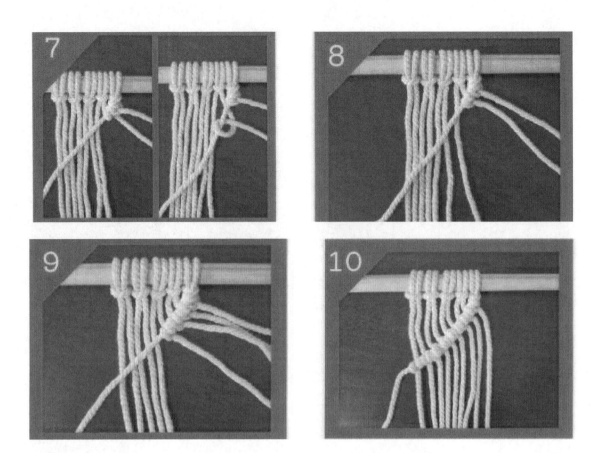

5.2 Techniques

You will need a few fundamental skills, which are described here, to finish the projects of macramé.

Mounting Techniques

When tying your knots, it is crucial to achieve solid tension, so prepare yourself beforehand by using the tips below.

A project board and T-pins are especially helpful for little tasks, like the clutch purse, where rope serves as the holding cord, or when crafting finer goods, like jewelry (see Tools & Materials). Alternatively, you can use adhesive tape to mount your holding cable to a wall, board, or another flat surface.

A clothing rack makes a perfect workstation for plant hangers or wall hangings where you mount your cords using a metal ring or dowel. Use S-hooks to hold these holding cords in place, or just connect your dowel or metal ring to the clothing rack's horizontal rail. Alternately, use two wall hooks to rest a piece of dowel on when creating a wall hanging or a single wall hook to hang a metal ring from when creating a plant hanger.

For wide-width projects, like our celebration arch, you can suspend your dowel from two sturdy wall hooks or a curtain rod, but be mindful of the wall hooks' ability to support their weight.

You can suspend your working project from a hook fixed into a ceiling beam for projects with a long vertical holding cord, like the hanging light or indoor swing, but make sure the hook's weight-bearing capacity is appropriate for your project.

Wrapping a Ring

Make a double half hitch with your length of rope and fasten one end of it to the metal ring. After threading the long end of the rope through the ring, wrap the rope around it fully, leaving just enough room for another double half hitch to hold it to the ring. Remove any extra cord.

Fraying

To create a fringe effect or a fuller tassel, the rope is unraveled using this finishing technique by dividing each strand into its component pieces.

Weaving Finish

A kind of finishing where the ends of the rope are neatly tucked below the knots on the back of the design.

Plaiting

Three cords or groups of cords are interlaced to form a braid by plaiting. To go from the center cord to the left cord, cross it over. The right cord should now be in the center after being crossed across the new center cord. To form the braid, keep alternating the left- and right-hand cords to the center position.

Numbering Cords

This is a method of counting cords to determine the precise place to start a macramé pattern. From left to right, cords are tallied; for smaller projects with fewer cables, this can be done mentally. It is simple to lose track of how many wires are being used when working on large projects. You can briefly tie a bit of colorful yarn around every tenth cord to aid in organization, or you can use pegs to keep clusters of cords together.

Lacing Up

By weaving the holding string through the openings in the alternating square knot patterns, the sides of the pocket on the clutch handbag are latched together.

Chapter 6: Plant Hangers

6.1 Three- or Four-Strand Base Design

Super modern, easy, and elegant. Only the overhand knot—the sole knot necessary for this plant hanger—needs to be mastered. This is basic, so the pattern may be enhanced later if desired or used as-is for a modern, silent hanger.

Working time: 20 to 25 minutes

Cords: 3–6mm–thick cotton, parachute cord, jute, polypropylene

Supplies:

Three-Strand Hanger

- (3) 7 ½'–8' (2.29–2.44m) the desired cord's lengths

Four-Strand Hanger

- (4) 8'–8 ½' (2.44–2.59m) the desired cord's lengths

Directions:

- Find the middle of the cotton cords and make a loop. Tie one large overhand knot at the end of the loop.

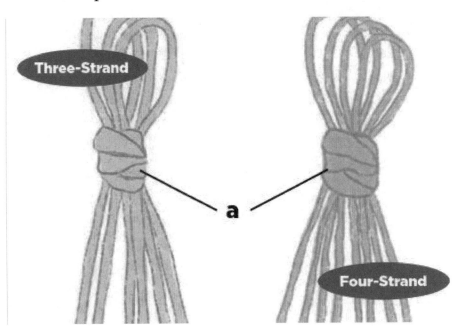

- Separate the strands into pairs and tie overhand knots in each pair 18" (45.72cm) from the large overhand knot.

- Separate two strands that are next to each other and tie an overhand knot about a palm's width (3 1/2 to 4 inches [8.89 to 10.16 cm]) from the first set of knots.

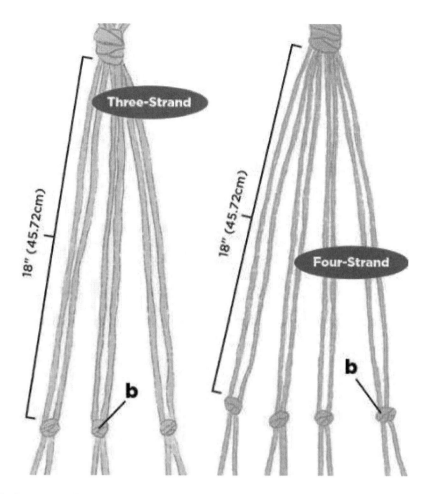

- Gather all the strands together and tie a big overhand knot 1 to 2 inches (2.54 to 5.08 cm) below the last row of knots.

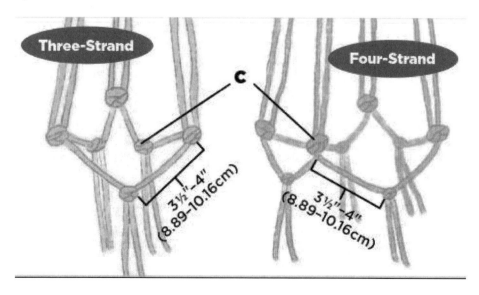

- If you want, you can even up the ends by trimming. This plant hanger is ready for a potted friend.

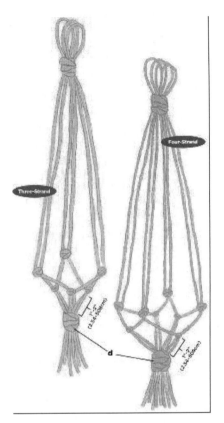

6.2 Wavy Embellishment Hanger

This pattern begins with a simple three-strand plant hanger. The square knot is given a variation in this project by the knotted pattern. The pattern you get from the design will be a zigzagging one rather than the blocked stripes you get from the Switch Knot Embellished Hanger.

Working time: 1.5 hours

Cords: 3–6mm–thick cotton, parachute cord, jute, polypropylene, worsted weight yarns, thread, strings, ribbon

Supplies:

- (3) 7' 6" (228.60cm) the desired cord's lengths

- (6) 6' (182.88) lengths of cotton crochet yarn in two colors

- A little amount of transparent, dry craft glue

Directions:

- Start by constructing the base of the three-strand plant hanger. Tie a huge overhand knot in the middle of the three thick cord strands. Use an overhand or square knot to join the two ends of two different colors of cotton yarn.

- Just below the topknot, center the cotton yarn knot behind two additional strands from the hanger and tie 12 half-knots.

- After that, tie a square knot (repeating the second half of the previous square knot). 12 half-knots should now be tied, rotating in the other direction.

- To make the half-knots flow in the opposite direction, repeat step 3 once more. Continue until the yarn cannot be tied into a knot any longer or until the sinnet measures approximately 8" (20.32 cm) in length. On the two dangling strands that are left, keep repeating this pattern.

- Cut off any extra cord, then dab some adhesive on the cut ends. Finish the hanger by following the instructions on the three-strand plant hanger foundation.

6.3 Double Herb Holder

Adding a little visual interest is this straightforward, sleek design. Want to hang a few herbs quickly? Not a problem. Additional splashes of color and textures are added to the plain plant hanger foundation, which is made of a strong, dense cotton cord.

Working time: 4 hours

Cords: Cotton, polypropylene, parachute cord, jute

Supplies:

- (4) 12' (3.66m) cotton rope in lengths (4mm)

- (12) 1' (30.48cm) lengths of vibrant jute twine (2mm)

- 7' (2.13m) length of vibrant jute twine

- 3' (91.44cm) long stretches of vibrant jute twine

Directions:

- Identify the cotton cords' center, then create a loop there. Cover a 4" (10.16cm) square with the 7" (2.13m) strand of vibrant jute portion with several square knots, and then reattach to create a loop.

- Form a row of alternate half-hitches using the separated cotton strands. "From the top loop, measure 14" (35.56cm).

- Form a second alternating half-hitch row of around three by re-pair-off the strands with the nearby strands "below the first by 3" (7.62) cm.

- One strand of vibrant 3" (91.44cm) jute should be used to gather all the strands and half-knot them. As a rule, wrap it between 2" and 3" (5.08 to 7.62 cm) below the second row of the alternate half-hitch row.

- Repetition of steps 2 through 4 starting at 20" (50.80cm) below the wrap.

- Use the remaining jute strands to embellish the hanger. Jute should be used to cover the cotton in square or half-knot patterns.

6.4 Ribbon Globe Hanger

A lightweight cactus, succulent, or air plant would work best for this project. A cute tiny chain could be created by the knot on its own. The ribbon highlights the plant hanger's presence and prevents it from blending in with its surroundings.

Working time: 2 hours

Cords: Ribbon, yarns, cotton string or twine, lightweight parachute cord, jute, acrylic cord, polypropylene

Supplies:

- 6' (182.88cm) length of 2"–3" (5.08–7.62cm) ribbon

- (2) 16' (4.88cm) jute lengths, with gauge thickness ranging from 1-2mm and two dissimilar colors (if the hole for the planter is large, use thicker strands)

- Glass globe succulent hanger

- Bit of clear-drying craft glue

- Metal hook (optional)

Directions:

- Place the ribbon onto the container, then secure the ends with an overhand knot. Alternatively, tie a lark's head knot. If you are worried about accidentally shattering the container while tying the knots, loop the ribbon into an optional metal hook so it may later be fastened to the hanger.

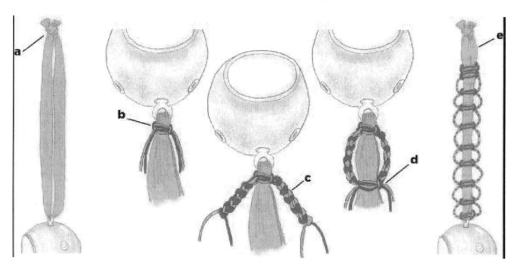

- At the bottom of the hanger, center the two strands of jute and tie an overhand knot.

- With each of the two cord combinations, create ten alternating half-hitches in succession. Wrap the ribbon with a single square knot.

- To reach the top of the hanger, repeat step three. Allow a few centimeters (a few inches) of space at the top for hanging. Finish the hanger by tying two square knots at the top. After trimming the excess jute, glue the cut points to keep them from fraying.

6.5 Lacy Ribbon Hanger

This plant hanger has a vintage feel thanks to the exquisite cream lace ribbon that was chosen for the project. This idea would also work nicely with a loudly printed ribbon because the rickrack edge will tone it down. This is a small plant stand that can securely hold a plant weighing between 8 and 12 ounces (226.80 and 340.19g).

Working time: 4 hours

Cords: Ribbon, yarns, cotton string or twine, acrylic cord, jute, polypropylene, lightweight parachute cord

Supplies:

- (2) 3' (91.44cm) lengths of ⅝"–1" (1.59–2.54cm) ribbon

- (8) 16' (4.88m) cotton crochet yarn lengths

- (2) 2' (60.96cm) cotton crochet yarn pieces

- Metal ring

- 4"–6" (10.16–15.24cm) plant holder

- Metal hook (optional)

- Bit of clear-drying craft glue

Directions:

- Onto the metal ring, center the ribbon and the 16' (4.88m) lengths of yarn. Just below the ring, wrap or tie several half-knots around the dangling strands using one 2' (60.96cm) length of yarn.

- Create three cord segments out of two strands of yarn knotted with 10 half-hitches each, a length of ribbon in the middle, and two additional pieces of yarn.

- Using two strands of yarn at a time, create a square around the ribbon. Wrap the ribbon with a single square knot. Between each square knot, there should be a 1" to 1 1/2" (2.54 to 3.81cm) space.

- Nearly 1/2" to 1" (1.27 to 2.54cm) or so from the ribbon's end, repeat step 3. Square knots are then tied around the ribbon. If the ribbon's end is frayed, slip the yarns so that there are two core strands in the center, then tie three to five square knots to fix it. On the three remaining dangling portions, repeat this procedure.

- About 2 1/2" to 3" (6.35 to 7.62cm) below the finished hanging wires, start creating the pot-holder sling. On the adjacent threads, tie a square knot. Set the alternate square knots from the previous row 1 1/2" to 2" (3.81 to 5.08cm) apart on the following row. Just below the second row, tie a big overhand knot after gathering up all the hanging threads. To the desired length, trim the ends.

6.6 Switch Knot Embellishment Hanger

This pattern begins with a simple three-strand plant hanger. The switch knots in contrasting colors will add a little more to your hanger. For the other colors, alternate between dark gray, black, and light gray while using a peachy pink on all three strands.

Working time: 2–3 hours

Cords: 3–6mm–thick cotton, worsted weight yarns, parachute cord, polypropylene, strings, jute, thread, ribbon

Supplies:

Three-Strand Hanger

- (3) 7' 6" (228.60cm) lengths of the desired rope (demonstrated utilizing 4mm cotton twist here)

Embellishments

- (6) 12' (3.66m) lengths of cotton crochet yarn in 4 different colors (3 in color A, 1 in color B, 1 in color C, and 1 in color D)

- A little amount of transparent, dry craft glue

Directions:

- A three-strand plant hanger base is created by gathering and cutting materials. One huge overhand knot should be made in the middle of the strands. The dangling strands should be paired off, and each pairing should be knotted overhand 18" (45.72cm) from the main overhand knot's base.

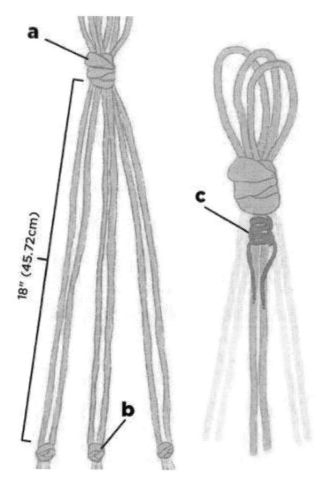

- Center the strands of color A and tie two square knots beginning at the top of the top knot.

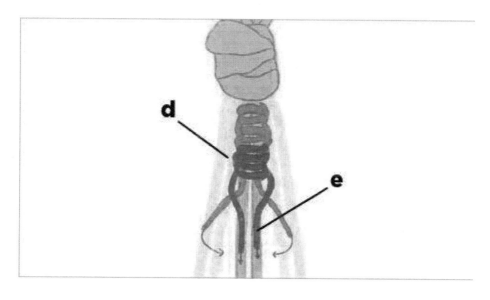

- Just below the final square knot, center the strands of color B, and create two square knots to enclose the entire hanging string. Form two square knots around the cluster with color A and tuck the strands of color B close to the hanger cords.

- For 12" (30.48cm), continue this alternate pattern. Use one strand of color A and one strand of color C on the following strand, then repeat on the other two hanging strands. Use one strand each of colors A and D for the third.

- The lower half (sling) of the hanger should be put together by the instructions for the three-strand basic hanger.

- Trim away any extra yarn before adding a little amount of glue to seal the cut points.

6.7 Raindrop Hanger

This lightweight piece is suggested for delicate planters or hanging lights. With the help of gravity, the suspension may extend and relax thanks to the alternating half-hitch. The colorful raindrops combine the planter and the plant, adding a touch of rustic appeal. Inspired in part by a string of pearl and jade succulents.

Working time: 2 hours

Cords: 1.5–2mm cotton string or twine, acrylic cord, jute, lightweight parachute cord, or 2mm polypropylene

Supplies:

Three-Strand Hanger

- (3) 7' 6" (228.60cm) lengths of the desired rope (demonstrated utilizing 4mm cotton twist here)

Embellishments

- Metal ring

- (4) 16' (4.88m) lengths of jute gauging about 1.5–2mm thickness

- Glass or light ceramic plant holder up to 8" (20.32cm) wide

- Bit of clear-drying craft glue

Directions:

- One huge overhand knot should be tied, butting up against the ring's base, with the four cord strands evenly spaced around the metal ring.

- A 4" to 6" (10.16 to 15.24 cm) sinnet of alternate half-hitches should be tied after pinning the strands in pairs (about 24 to 40 alternating half-hitches).

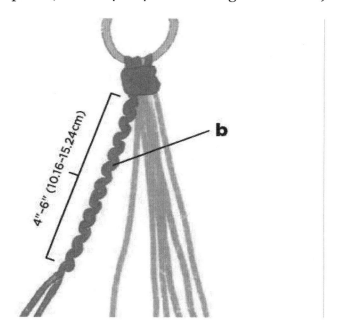

- To fix the teardrop shape, fold up roughly 2" (5.08cm) and tie a square knot over the sinnet. Another 4" to 6" of the sinnet strand should be added (10.16 to 15.24cm). As desired, create 3 or 4 "raindrops."

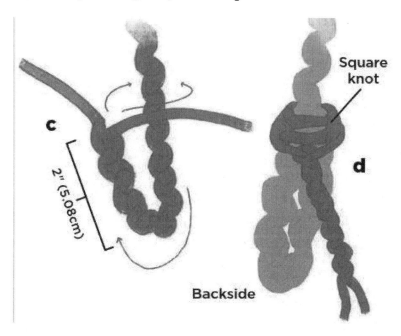

- Apply the teardrop pattern consistently until the sinnet is about 18" long (45.72cm). Follow the same procedure for the final three chord pairs. The hanger will look more natural if the "raindrop" placements are staggered from strand to strand.

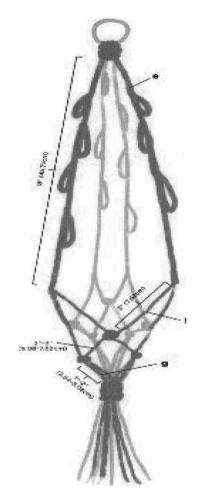

- About 3" (7.62 cm) below the half-hitch sinnets form the sling. Use an overhand knot or an alternating half-hitch to join one strand from each neighboring hanging thread. This project was completed with these techniques. Finish by gathering all the strands at the base and tying a sizable overhand knot 1" to 2" (2.54 to 5.08cm) from the previous row. Next, form the opposite row 2" to 3" (5.08 to 7.62cm) below.

- Cut the dangling fringe to the length you want. To stop fraying, clear-drying glue can be applied to the fringe's tips.

6.8 Stitched Plant Hanger

Any material may be used to create this plant hanger. For the tiny and one of the larger hangers, use a 2mm jute, and for the huge hanger, use a 4mm polypropylene braid. To help with the rustic appearance, some of the jute was hand-painted. This project is particularly unique in that it just calls for one knot to perform the entire task.

Working time: 1–2 hours

Cords: 4–6mm cords (braided or twisted), jute, polypropylene, cotton, or nylon

Supplies:

Small Hanger:

- Metal or wooden ring
- (2) 4' (121.92cm) neutral cord pieces A
- (4) 7' (213.36cm) neutral cord pieces A
- (2) 4' (121.92cm) fragments of vibrant cord B
- (2) 2' (60.96cm) fragments of vibrant cord B

Large Hanger:

- Metal or wooden ring
- (2) 8' (243.84cm) neutral cord pieces A
- (4) 14' (426.72cm) neutral cord pieces A
- (2) 8' (243.84cm) pieces of vibrant cord B
- (2) 2' (60.96cm) pieces of vibrant cord B

Directions:

- The two 2' (60.96cm) lengths of the cord should be set aside. Onto the ring, place the remaining rope pieces in the middle. It could be simpler to center the longer pieces first, followed by the shorter ones.

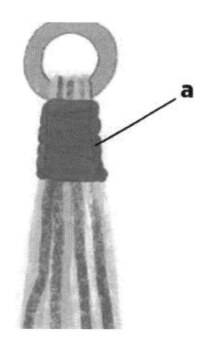

- A square knot should be made around the bundle after positioning one of the 2' (60.96cm) lengths of cord directly underneath the ring. The hanging parts will be fixed in place as a result. Till you run out of cord, square knot, snip off any extra, stray strands.

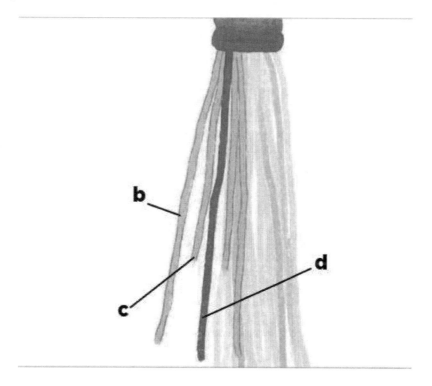

- Separate and organize the first hanging line so that it has one long neutral strand in the center, two long neutral strands on either side, and two shorter neutral strands after that.

- Use the lengthy outside threads to tie five square knots. Together with the neutral cord, advance the colored strand and tie three more square knots. Make five more square knots on top of the colorful cord by sliding it back into the center. To make a little hanger, repeat this step once more. To construct a long hanging, repeat this step four more times.

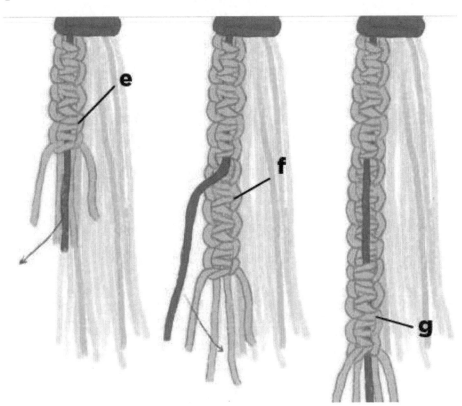

- On the remaining portions, repeat steps 3 and 4.

- Form the basket sling once you have all four hanging strands finished. Create two rows of alternating square knots, each about three "7'62" apart. Form two rows of alternating square knots measuring 5 inches apart for the large hanger "12 70 cm apart.

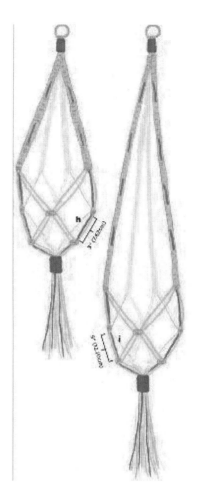

- A few millimeters (or a few inches) below the final row of knots gather all the strands together. Create another set of square knots while centering the final piece of vibrant cord. Trim the extra material.

- Cut the hanger fringe to the desired length.

6.9 Twinkle Plant Hanger

Sparkles without any fringe? Yep! This tiny hanger is made to be viewed at any time of day or night. The appearance of falling stars is created. For mess-free access to the on/off switch, it is advisable to use this hanger in conjunction with artificial plants.

Keep the plant profile tiny and light; plants under 2 lbs. (0.91 kg) and 6" (15.24 cm) are excellent. While the weight is supported by the jute alone, the string of lights is very light. Only half-knots and overhand knots are used in this project, but maintaining the level of the light strands as the knots are installed is a difficult balancing act.

Working time: 3 hours

Cords: 2mm cords, cotton braid or twist, polypropylene, jute, nylon, or worsted weight yarn in acrylic or cotton

Supplies:

- Metal or wooden ring

- (4) 8' (2.44cm) neutral cord pieces A

- (4) 8' (2.44cm) neutral cord pieces B

- (2) Battery-operated light strings (10' [3.05m] string) plus batteries

- 6" (15.24cm) planter with a central drainage hole

- Clear-drying glue

- Tape

Directions:

- To prevent it from escaping through the bottom of the pot, gather all the jute and transfer it through the planter's drainage hole before tying one sizable overhand knot.

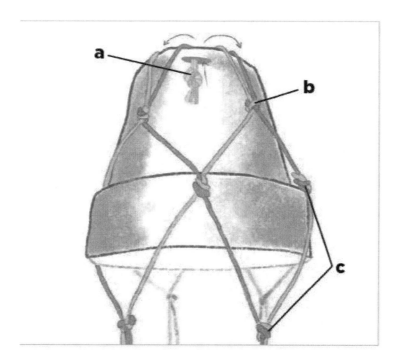

- Pair off the jute strands to create the netting while still holding the planter upside down. By the base of the planter, create a row of overhand knots.

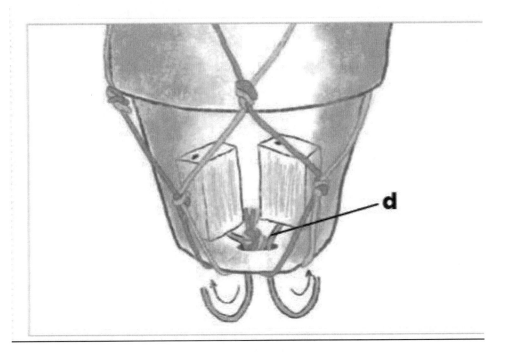

- Reassemble the jute to create two more rows of alternate overhand knots.

- TIP: To prevent the net from moving when the pot is turned upright, gather all the jute and temporarily create a big overhand knot.

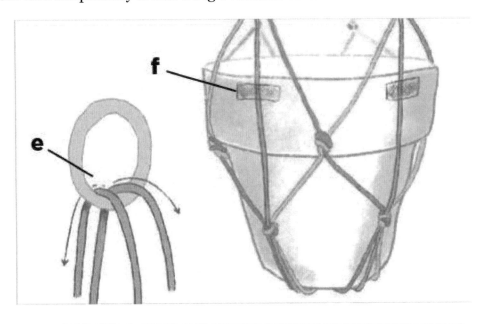

- Turn the planter upside down, then feed the two strings of lights from the inside through the drainage hole.

- Tape the light strands in place all around the planter after threading the light strands through the metal ring and locating their centers. The two plastic-covered, unlit portions of the strands should be placed opposite one another on the pot, and the two lit portions should be in the same position.

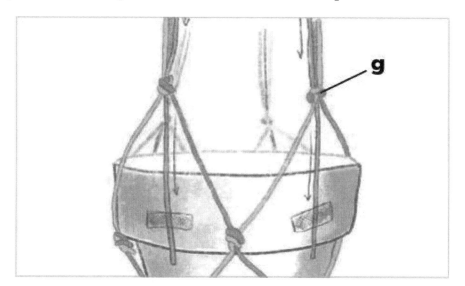

- For each pair of jute string knots to line up with a strand of lights, adjust the netting. Starting just above the pot's lip, tie 10 half-knots around the light strands.

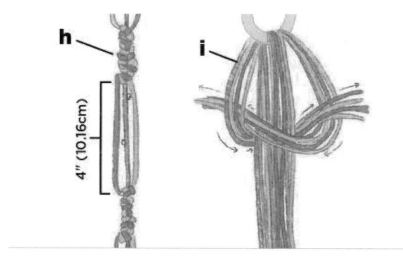

- Laying the planter on its side might be helpful. Every 4", Make ten half-knots along each light strand (10.16cm). Allow the final 6 to 8 inches (15.24 to 20.32 cm) to be knot-free.

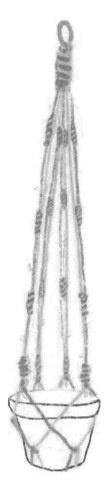

- Once all of the strands are coated, feed the jute through the metal ring and secure the hanging by tying a thick half-knot sinnet. Make a thick square knot about 3" in length (7.62 cm).

6.10 Air Plant Hanger

An air plant that seeks a little freedom and vitality has found a home here. This sea urchin-inspired air plant container can be obtained at a neighborhood garden center. These are easily accessible online and at a few neighborhood craft shops. You can even utilize actual shells. It is possible to lightly paint the ceramic holder to complement the style of your home.

Working time: 2–4 hours

Cords: Yarns, cotton string or twine, jute, lightweight parachute cord, acrylic cord, polypropylene

Supplies:

- Metal ring

- (2) 8 yd. (7.32m) lengths of jute with a thickness of roughly 1-2 mm (if the planter's hole is especially large, utilize thicker material) in two different hues

- 4' (1.22m) piece of jute

- Ceramic air plant stand or a tiny inverted container made of terracotta

- Bit of transparent-drying craft glue

Directions:

- The 4' (121.92cm) piece of the cord should be tied to the ring using a lark's head knot, and the ends should be threaded into the air plant holder. Use an overhand knot to join them. Enter the planter with the knot. This will serve as the half knots' central point.

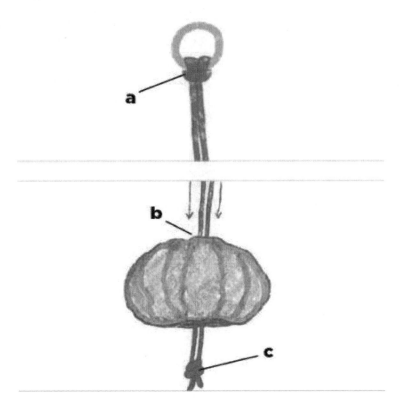

- Just above the planter, center and half-knot the remaining two cords into the core. The cords should be arranged now, with matched colors mirroring one another on either side of the core to create an "X" shape.

- Make a half-knot with the color A. Put the strands out of the path and use color B to tie a half-knot.

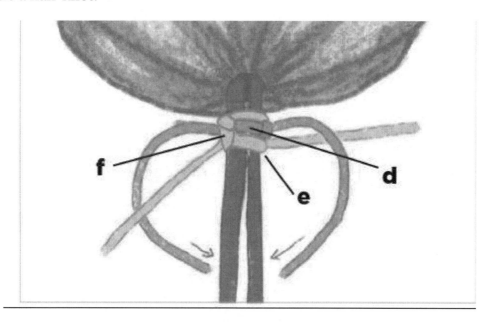

- Up until you reach the ring, keep alternating half-knots in place. e.

- Trim the extra cord and join the raw ends with a little amount of clear, fast-drying glue.

Chapter 7: Mats

7.1 Ultra-Plush Mat

This mat is a great way to soften the look of any room. You might also think about putting it by your bed. In the morning, picture burying your toes into this fluffy piece.

This mat seems cozy. Oh yes! Is making it simple? Absolutely. Only the Josephine knot has to be mastered for this project. For a beginner, this knot could be a little challenging to manage in sinnet form, but with practice, this rug is simple to master.

Working time: 8–12 hours

Cords: Incredibly thick acrylic yarns

Supplies:

- About 100 yds. (91.44m) incredibly thick acrylic yarn (¾"–1" [1.91–2.54cm] round)

- Crochet hook (optional)

Directions:

- Cut the yarn into seven pieces that are 19' (5.79m) long and nine pieces that are 16' (4.88m) long.

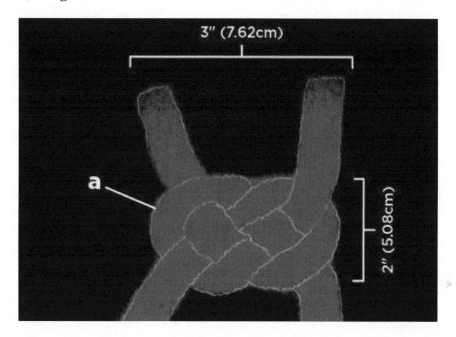

- Utilizing two 16' (4.88m) strands of yarn, tie a Josephine knot. This knot ought to rest around 2" (5.08 cm) from the very end. Each knot needs to be 2" tall and 3" wide (5.08 by 7.62cm).

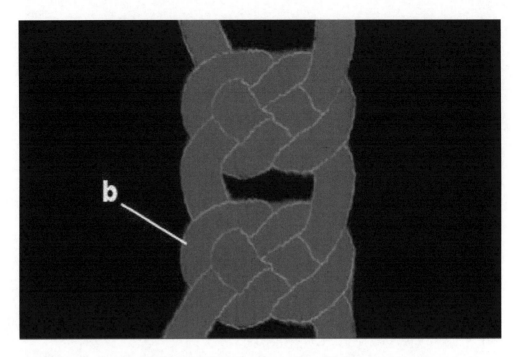

- TIP: If any strands were knotted together, the bulky knots might be readily hidden in the center of the knot.

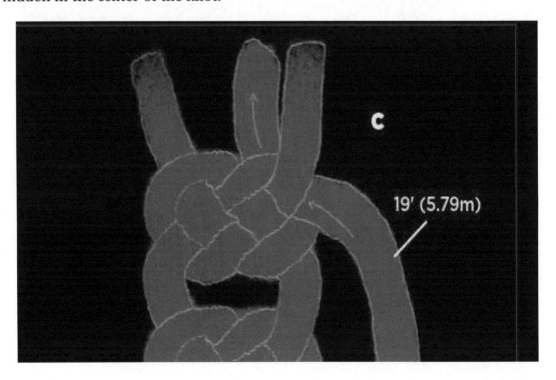

- Josephine knots should be formed in a sinnet until the length is 4' (121.92 cm) or 50 "127 cm.

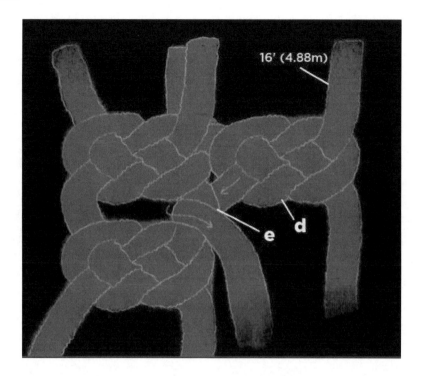

- Collect the following two strands, measuring 19" and 16" (5.79 and 4.88m). Before tying the two core ends together, thread the 19' (5.79m) strand through the first Josephine knot that has been made. The two sinnets will be stitched together and secured as a result.

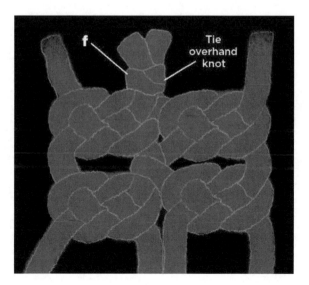

- On this column, tie the first Josephine knot. Thread the left (longer) strand through the second knot from the first column before tying the second knot.

- This pattern should be repeated until the throw is 2" by 4" (60.96 by 121.92cm) wide. Tie the loose ends together and weave the extra yarn into the throw to complete it.

7.2 Patch Scrap Mat

Use all those fabric leftovers from your stockpile with this vibrant and cheerful rug. The beauty of this mat is in the haphazard placement of fabric scrap! Pinking shears could be used to create a zigzag pattern on the edges of the fabric scraps if you wanted something a bit more beautiful (and to stop them from fraying).

Working time: 3 hours

Cords: Scrap fabric or ribbon

Supplies:

- Roughly 250'–300' (76.20–91.44m) of scrap fabric pieces, each 1"–1 ½" (2.54–3.81cm) wide

- 9' x 1" (274.32 x 2.54cm) length of fabric (or ribbon, or several fabrics tied together)

- 30" x 18" (76.20 x 45.72cm) non-slip mat (optional)Paper clip-based wire hook or crochet hook

- T-pin-enhanced macramé board (optional)

Directions:

- Pin the 9" (2.74m) fabric strip into a rectangle that measures 30" by 18" (76.20 by 45.72cm) (ideally on a large surface or macramé board). To enable these pieces to be knotted together, leave at least a 6" (15.24cm) overhang at the starting and end of each piece.

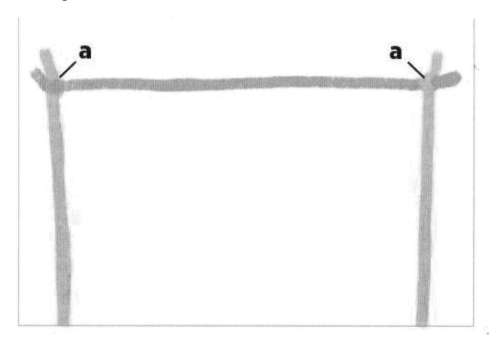

- With a clove hitch, attach 40 pieces to the rectangle's top.

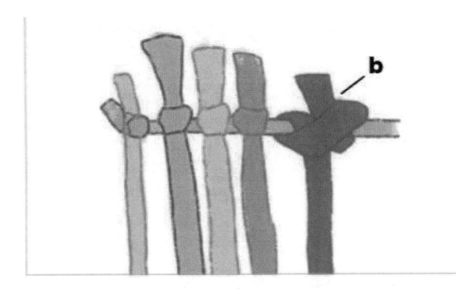

- Wrap the first piece of cloth around the rectangle's left edge, starting at the left. Cross strips 4 and 5, then use the four hanging pieces of cloth to tie a square knot.

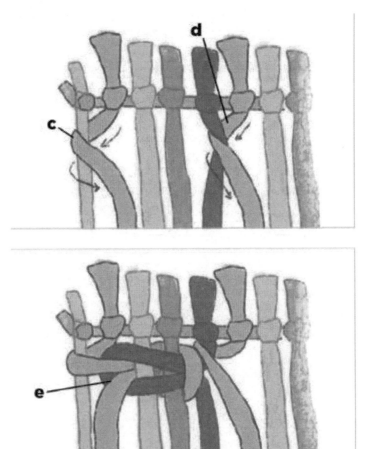

- Twist the fourth and fifth pieces further, then tie square knots across the row. Form the final square knot by encircling the right edge with the last piece of fabric at the end of the row.

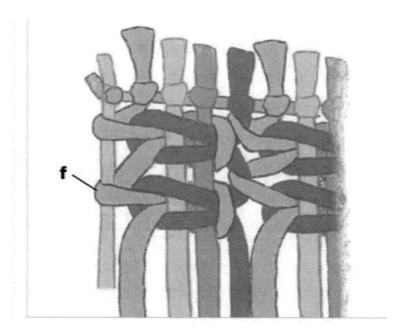

- TIP: To keep the mat straight, pin each row as you finish it.

- To fill in the mat, repeat steps 3 and 4. Add more fabric to the end as the pieces get shorter.

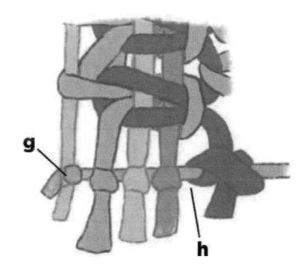

- Tie in a fresh bottom anchor piece to complete. Attach each piece of cloth with a clove hitch to the underside of the new anchor piece. If a completed edge is desired, use a hook to weave ends into the mat's bottom. If you intend to use the mat as a welcome mat, place it on a non-slip surface.

7.3 Honeycomb Mat

This substantial mat is a wonderful way to add style to any tabletop. You can use a cord with a variety of gentle hues that complement one another well. A charming pattern that adds interest to any décor is the holey pattern. This mat is the ideal size for a coffee table, but you might want to double its size so that it can be used as a rug at your front entrance.

Working time: 6 hours

Cords: 4–6 mm polypropylene cord or 4 mm jute

Supplies:

- 278' (84.73m) of 6mm polypropylene cord cut into:

- 38' (11.58m) length (perimeter piece)

- (10) 24' (7.32m) lengths

- A tiny crochet hook or a hook-shaped piece of floral wire

- Cork or foam board (at least 2' x 3' [60.96 x 91.44cm] wide) with T-pins

Directions:

- Fold the 38' (11.58m) piece of cord in half, then knot it in a series of alternating half-hitches beginning at the mat's edge. With two short sides and one long side, the chain's total length should be 56" (1.42m).

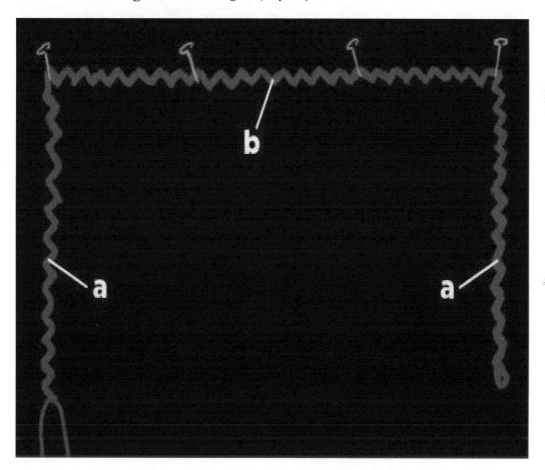

- TIP: Form infinite bundles to keep the lengthy lengths under control.

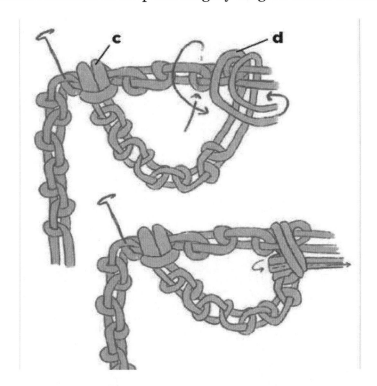

- Incorporate the partial rectangle by tacking the half-hitch strip down. When the last row is formed, the remaining cord will be knotted.

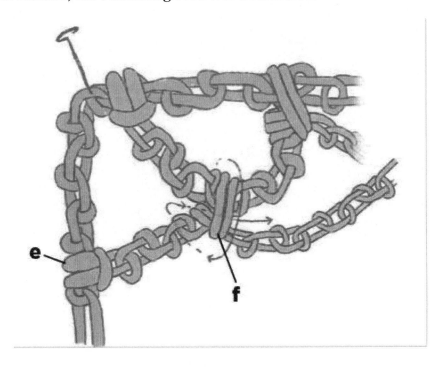

- Take a piece of cord that is 24" (7.32m) long and fold it in half. One mat corner should be tied with a lark's head knot. To finish this row, make eight alternate half-hitches, loop to the mat's top from the back, and then repeat across the width of the mat. When the mat is finished, the ends will be woven back in.

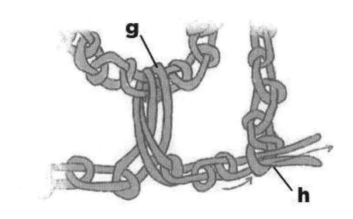

- Take another strand of cord and, parallel to the bottom of the first loop on the following row, tie a lark's head knot to the mat's vertical edge. Hitch at the bottom of the first loop after making four alternate half-hitches. Making eight alternate half-hitches across this row, tack to the bottom of the scale from the row before.

- For the remainder of the mat until the final row, repeat steps 3 and 4 for rows 1 and 2.

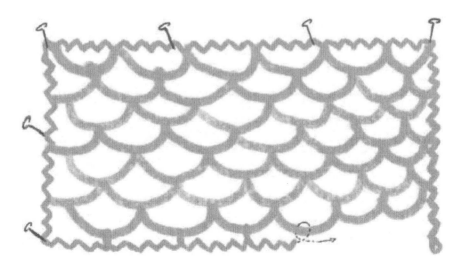

- The last row is created by going back to the outer hanging strand and making four alternate half-hitches before binding with the bottom peak of the row before. Form eight alternate half-hitches, then tie a binding across the row, leaving only four knots remaining at the end.

- Pass the ends through the perimeter weave's bottom to complete. Tie off using an alternate half-hitch, trim the ends, then, if you would like, melt (with polypropylene cord alone) the cut ends. It might be necessary to block this mat (keep it nailed to a board for a day or more) for it to take on its final shape.

Chapter 8: Home Décor

8.1 Hanging Shelf

It is a great idea to put light things on this elegant shelf unit. It can be hung from the ceiling or the wall against a wall. It is suspended from a sixteen-cord half-knot spiral, which makes it perfect for any room in your house. Just make sure you use a plug & screw that can hold at least ten kg (22 lb. Please keep in mind that the sort of plug and screw you need will depend on how your wall is built, how heavy the shelves are, and what will be on them.

Working time: 3 to 4 hours

Supplies:

- 74m (242 1/2 ft.) 5 mm in length (1/4 in) rope

- 8cm (3 1/8 in) metal ring

- Two pieces of pine wood, each 48cm (19in) long, 18.5cm (7 1/4 in) wide, and 2cm (3/4 in) thick

- 120 grit (fine) sandpaper

- Drill with a wood drill bit with a 15mm (19/32 in) diameter

- Wood stain in your preferred color

Preparation:

- Cut 8 pieces of 5mm (1/4 in) rope that are 9m (29 1/2 ft.) long

- Lightly sand the wood to get rid of any rough or uneven surfaces, then stain it your preferred shade

- Cut one 2m (6 1/2 ft.) length of 5mm (1/4 in) rope

- Mark a hole in each corner of every piece of wood 2 cm (3/4 in) from the edge, then drill the holes

Directions:

- The 8cm (3 1/8 in) metal ring needs to be wrapped with the 2m (6 1/2 ft.) piece of rope.

- You can install the eight 9m (29 1/2 ft.) rope lengths onto the ring by bending them in half over the interior of the ring.

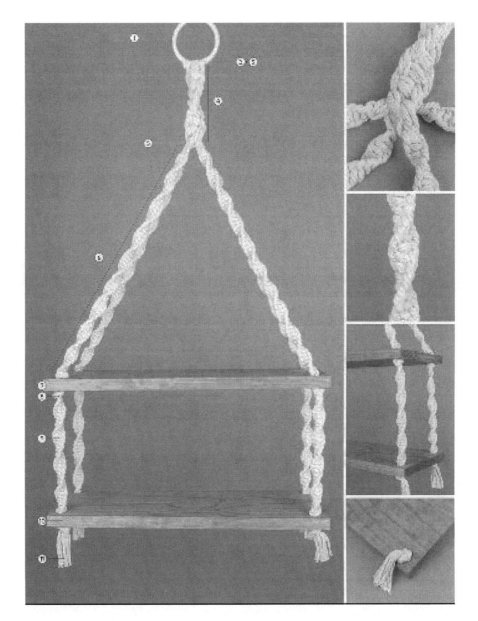

- Sort the cords into three groups: group 3 has four cords, group 2 has eight cords, and group 1 has four cords.

- Use group 1 & group 3 cords as working cords, group 2 cords as the filler cords, and eight half knots to tie a sixteen-cord half-knot spiral.

- Four groups of 4 cords each will now be created from the cords.

- With 64 half knots each for the 4 groups, tie a four-cord half-knot spiral and lower it by 1.5 cm (5/8 in).

- Place the first shelf horizontally & thread a string through each of the spiral's four corner holes.

- Flip the shelf over and make an overhand knot in each bundle of cords to hold the shelf at each corner. Before continuing, flip the shelf upside-down to ensure it is level after forming the final four knots.

- Right beneath every overhand knot, tie a four-cord half-knot spiral using 32 half knots for each of the 4-cord groups.

- Repeat steps number 7 and 8

- Trim the cords to 5.5 cm (2 1/4 in), then fray them.

8.2 Cushion Decoration

Add a stunning macramé panel to a plain cushion cover to transform it. The panel is formed from an alternating square knot design with a focal bead insertion. Your cushion top is hand-sewed to the finished panel. Why not try building others in various sizes and shapes once you have perfected the first one? Hand cleaning is advised because we have selected a natural calico cover to match the natural cotton rope precisely.

Working time: 3 hours

Supplies:

- 54.7m (182 1/2 ft.) length of 5mm (1/4 in) rope

- 3 wooden beads, 2.5cm (1in) long x 2cm (3/4 in) wide with a 1cm (3/8 in) hole

- 40 x 40cm (16 x 16in) cushion case and insert

- Hot glue gun

Preparation:

- Cut two 35cm (13 3/4 in) lengths of 5mm (1/4 in) rope

- Cut eighteen 3m (10ft) lengths of 5mm (1/4 in) rope

Directions:

- One of the 35cm (13 3/4 in) lengths of rope should be fastened straight and firmly to a project board using T-pins (or to a flat surface using adhesive tape). You can use this as a holding cord.

- Reverse lark's head knots should be used to attach the eighteen 3 m (10 ft.) lengths of rope to the holding cord, centering them so that there is about 6-7 cm (2 3/8 -2 3/4 in) of uncovered holding cord at each end. The mounted rope should have a width of about 22 cm (8 5/8 in).

- Tie nine square knots directly behind the row of reverse lark's head knots.

- Alternate the cords, then tie an eight-square-knot row.

- Seven more rows of alternating square knots should be worked.

- Number the ropes from 1 to 36. Tie a square knot with cords 3-6 and another square knot with cords 7-10 directly beneath the final row of square knots.

- To make a wooden bead sit directly against the square knot above it, thread it onto cords 14 and 15.

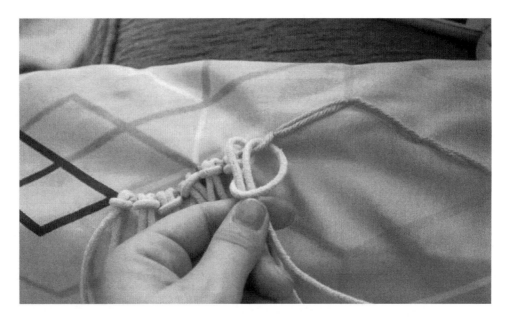

- To make a wooden bead sit directly against the square knot above it, thread it onto cords 18 and 19.

- To make a wooden bead sit directly against the square knot above it, thread it onto cords 22 and 23.

- Tie a square knot with cords 27–30, then a second square knot with cords 31–34 in line with the row.

- Renumber the cords from 1 to 36 again. Tie square knots with cords 1-4, 5-8, and 9-12, as well as with cords 25-28, 29-32, and 33-36, to form a new row. This row of square knots should now be parallel to the bottom of the beads.

- Tie a row of eight square knots right below, alternating the cords.

- Seven further rows of alternating square knots should be tied using different ropes.

- Place the remaining 35 cm (13 3/4 in) of rope over all the cords, ensuring the ends are even on both sides. As of right now, this will serve as the holding cord.

- Trim all of the cords to 3 cm (1 1/8 in) after half-hitching them to the holding cord.

- At the ends of the holding cords, make a tight overhand knot, ensuring the knot is tightly pressed against the edges of your work. The holding ropes should be cut to 4 cm (1 1/2 in).

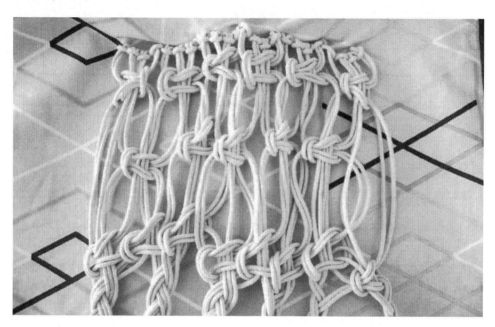

- The cord ends should all be adhered to the back of the macramé panel by flipping it over and using the hot glue gun.

- Hand-sew the macramé panel to the front of your cushion cover from the right side.

8.3 Deck Chair

With this macramé design, you can transform a standard deck chair into a custom piece of furniture. To make your masterpiece, just take the fabric off the deck chair's frame and follow the design. You may need to adapt the length and width of the macramé panel to fit if your deck chair is a different size from the one we used, making the adjustments necessary to make it the same size as the original deck chair fabric.

Working time: 4 to 5 hours

Supplies:

- 304m (997 1/2 ft.) length of 5mm (1/4 in) rope

- Hot glue gun

- Deck chair frame 88cm (35 3/4 in) high x 97cm (38 1/8 in) wide x 67cm (26 3/8 in) deep

Preparation:

- Cut thirty-eight 8m (26 1/4 ft.) lengths of 5mm (1/4 in) rope

- Remove the existing fabric from the frame of the deck chair with caution

Directions:

- Reverse lark's head knots should be used to attach all thirty-eight 8m (26 1/4 ft) pieces of rope to the top bar of the deck chair frame, ensuring that the cords are evenly spaced apart. The mounted rope's breadth should be roughly 47 cm (18 1/2 in) (or the width of the original fabric).

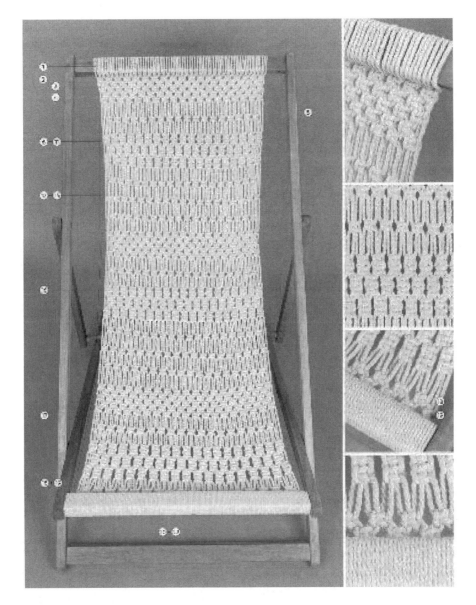

- To hold the cords in place, tie a row of 19 square knots just beneath.

- Alternate the cords just below and tie a row of 18 square knots.

- Three more rows of alternating square knots, with no space in between, should be continued.

- Alternate the cords, 3.5 cm (1 3/8 in) down, and tie a row of 18 square knots.

- Alternate the cords, then make a row of nineteen square knots at a height of 3.5 cm (1 3/8 in).

- 19 square knots in a row should be tied directly beneath.

- Tie a row of eighteen square knots using alternating cords.

- 18 square knots in a row should be tied directly beneath.

- Tie a row of nineteen square knots using alternating cords.

- 19 square knots in a row should be tied directly beneath.

- Alternate the cords, 3.5 cm (1 3/8 in) down, and tie a row of 18 square knots.

- Alternate the cords, then make a row of nineteen square knots at a height of 3.5 cm (1 3/8 in).

- Alternate the cords, 3.5 cm (1 3/8 in) down, and tie a row of 18 square knots.

- Alternate the cords, then make a row of nineteen square knots at a height of 3.5 cm (1 3/8 in).

- Steps 3 through 15 should be repeated.

- Steps 3 through 11 should be repeated.

- Alternate the cords, then tie a row of 18 square knots at a height of 3 cm (1 1/8 in).

- Alternate the cords just below and tie a row of 19 square knots.

- Now, fasten the macramé panel to the deck chair's bottom bar by bringing all of the cords underneath the bottom bar and tying a double half-hitch knot around each rope. Before fastening the macramé panel to the chair's bottom bar, make sure it has been drawn extremely tightly so that it will not have too much give when in use.

- Once all cords are fastened to the bottom bar, draw them as far as you can in the direction of the chair's underside and tie them in pairs using double overhand knots, counting 1 and 2, 3 and 4, 5 and 6, 7 and 8, and so forth.

- Use the hot glue gun to flatten the cord ends after trimming them to a length of about 5mm (1/4 in).

8.4 Tutu Chandelier

The capiz shell and tassel chandeliers in home decor shops served as the inspiration for this project. Untwisted cotton's ribbon-like waves have a texture similar to that of real seagrass. This project has a classic, shabby chic atmosphere that will always go with a bohemian room's decor when paired with the current inverted tier.

For this project, we went with a light blush pink tint. Although this may be done in any color, you can think of. We advise using mint, cream, and soft corals to maintain the mermaid-like femininity of the design.

Working time: 8 to 12 hours

Cords: Yarns, cotton string, or twine

Supplies:

- 8" (20.32cm) metal ring

- Portable lamp kit

- Light bulb

- Lampshade, at least 10" (25.40cm) at the top

- Approximately 140 yds. (128.02m) cotton crochet yarn in the color of your preference (measures around ⅛" [0.32cm] in diameter)

- Macramé brush (recommended)

Directions:

- Cut the cotton yarn into lengths of 12" (30.48 cm). This will require some time! The final parts required are 240 for the larger ring and 176 for the smaller ring. To make them ready to grab and simple to count, pile eight pieces together for each triangular shape on the rings.

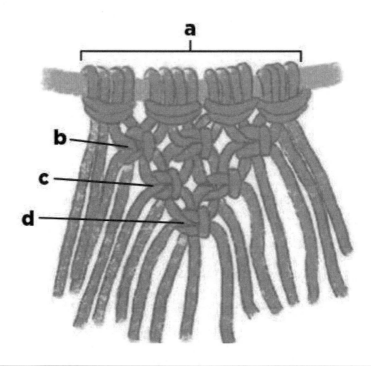

- Take the lampshade apart. The larger base of the lamp was placed aside to be used for a future dream catcher project and used only the top piece of the light.

- To secure each piece to the rings, tie a double lark's head knot: Assemble 240 parts for the 10" (25.40cm) ring and 176 pieces for the 8" (20.32cm) ring. Note: we advise mounting eight parts (four full double lark's head knots) at once, then continuing with the knot-tying procedure. This will make it simpler to organize and follow the detailed work.

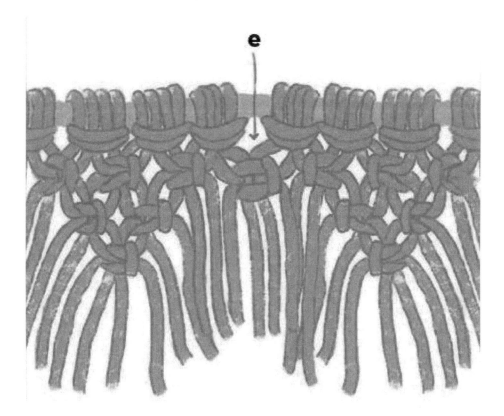

- Create three alternating square knots starting with one of the rings. Create two alternating square knots by moving down one row. Next, lower one row, and tie a square knot. Repetition is necessary along the ring's perimeter.

- To join the pieces together as you work your way around the ring, make a square knot; this will stop the string from slipping between the lark's head knots. This keeps the pieces separate and makes organization easier.

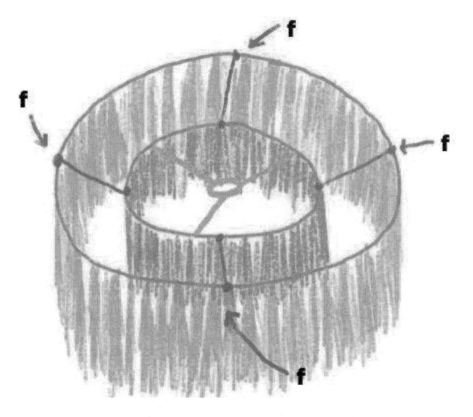

- To fluff up the fringe, untwist the yarn strands and comb them through with your fingers or a macramé brush. Use the brush to comb the hair gently, beginning at the bottom of the strand and moving up toward the knots.

- To mount and tie the string onto the remaining ring, repeat steps 4 through 6.

- Do you want to expand this project? To keep the ring completely wrapped, add sixteen strands (eight double lark's head knots) for every inch (2.54 cm) in diameter over that.

- The 10" (25.40cm) ring should be in the center of the 8" (20.32cm) ring. Connect the rings with four to six pieces of yarn. Holding the 10" (25.40cm) ring level, measure the 8" (20.32cm) ring's balance.

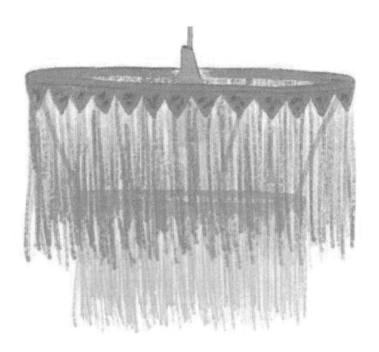

- Add the light bulb and fasten the lamp kit to the 10" (25.40cm) ring. Hang and activate your gorgeous piece of artwork!

- TIP: For the lampshade and kit, we suggest visiting your neighborhood home improvement retailer. Most people will already have the necessary components for this simple project.

8.5 Amazing Macramé Curtain

Your home will have a beach house ambiance thanks to macramé curtains. You are not even required to add any shells or trinkets, but you can if you like.

Here is a fantastic macramé curtain that you can build, however.

Working time: 3 to 5 hours

Cords: Yarns, cotton string, or twine

Supplies:

- Laundry rope (or any kind of rope/cord you want)

- Scissors

- Curtain rod

- Lighter

- Pins

- Tape

Directions:

- Four strands should be tied together, and the top knots should be pinned to keep the structure in place.

- Take the strand on the outer right section, pass it through the middle, and let it cross over to the left side. Reverse after tightly pulling the ropes together.

- For the thread you now have in front of you, repeat crossing it over four more times. Take the outer-left strand and allow it to cross over the center. Next, take the right strand and allow it to cross over the outer-left strand. Continue as necessary, then divide the collection of strands to the left and the right. Continue until you get the desired number of rows.

- This can now be used on the ropes. Gathering the desired number of ropes—10 to 14 is acceptable, or however, many fit the rod with adequate spacing.

- Beginning at the curtain's top, tie knots until the length you want is reached. To keep the ends from unraveling, burn or tape them.

- To give the ropes that enchanting seashore appearance, braid them together.

- You can now utilize your new curtain after that.

8.6 Hanging Photo Gallery

A charming dorm room delight is created when form and functionality come together. The idea behind this framework is that it can be used as a straightforward piece of room décor on its own or that it can be personalized with photos and jewelry. For knot practice, this is a visually lovely creation.

Working time: 3 to 5 hours

Cords: Worsted 1mm leather, weight yarns, 1mm satin rattail cord

Supplies:

- (20) 2 ½' (76.20cm) cotton crochet yarn lengths

- (4) 8' (2.44m) cotton crochet yarn lengths

- Approximately 100' (30.48m) of cotton crochet yarn for the feathers

- (4) 20' (6.10m) cotton crochet yarn lengths

- Macramé board with the T-pins (recommended)

- (12+) Decorative paper clips or tiny binder clips

- Glue

- (4+) Wall tacks or clear plastic micro wall mount clips

Directions:

- Tie four lengths of the 2 1/2" (76.20cm) cords together by placing an overhand knot 3" (7.62cm) from one end, starting with the horizontal bars. Continue to braid four strands for 18" (45.72 cm), ending with another overhand knot. Five horizontal pieces in total should be made.

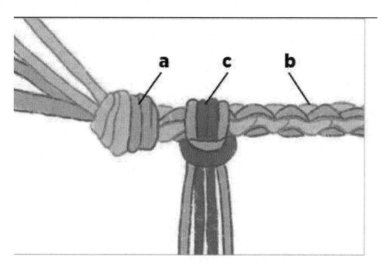

- Find the centers of two lengths of yarn: one 8" (2.44m) and one 20" (6.10m), then tie a double lark's head knot to the end of one of the braids when it is finished. To serve as the core for the square knots formed with the green yarn, the blue yarn must be in the center.

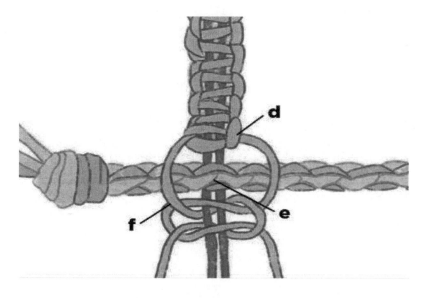

- 6" square knot (15.24cm). Slip the braided rope, so it is in front of the core and start the first half of a square knot to add the next horizontal bar. Tighten after completing the other side of the square knot. Once all five braided sections have been mounted, continue by making another 6" (15.24cm) sinnet of square knots. Finish the last mount by tying an overhand knot, then a square knot.

- For the following three vertical mounts, repeat steps 2 and 3, spacing each bar 6" (15.24cm) apart.

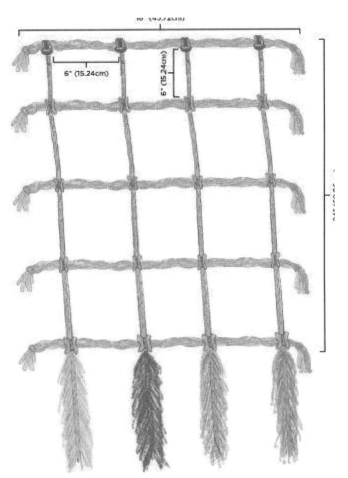

- Forming feathers at the hanging's base and reducing the side tassels to 3" will complete the project (7.62cm). Here, each feather is made using 24' (7.32m) of yarn that has been divided into 6" (15.24cm) segments.

- Tacks or detachable transparent micro wall clips can be used to hang the frame from a wall. Pictures and small decorations can be added to the frame using little binder clips or colorful paper clips.

8.7 Indoor Swing

In addition to adding charm and character to your home, an incredibly elegant indoor swing also serves as a terrific way to add some extra sitting. This unique piece of furniture is ideal for a variety of home types thanks to the half-knot spiral handles made of natural cotton rope that fork at the base to link to a sturdy hardwood seat.

Working time: 7 hours

Cords: Worsted 1mm leather, weight yarns, 1mm satin rattail cord

Supplies:

- 258m (846 1/2 ft.) length of 5mm (1/4 in) rope

- Two sizable carabiners in zinc plating

- Two 8cm (3 1/8 in) zinc-plated metal rings, heavy-duty (6mm/ 1/4 in)

- One pine wood piece, measuring 48cm (19in) long x 18.5cm (7 1/4 in) wide x 3cm (1 1/8 in) high

- Drill with a 15mm (19/32 in) wood drill bit

- Use your favorite color of wood stain

- 180 grit (very fine) sandpaper

Preparation:

- Cut two 1m (3 1/4 ft.) lengths of 5mm (1/4 in) rope

- In each of the wood's corners, mark a hole position 2cm (3/4 in) from the sides and drill the holes next

- Cut sixteen 16m (52 1/2 ft.) lengths of 5mm (1/4 in) rope

- After lightly sanding the wood to get rid of any rough or uneven areas, stain it the color you want

Directions:

- Folding the rope in half over the inside of the ring will allow you to mount eight 16m (52 1/2 foot) lengths of rope onto one of the metal rings.

- One of the 1m (3 1/4 ft.) pieces of rope should be used to tie a 4 cm (1 1/2 in) wrapped knot around each cord.

- Sort the cords into three groups that are four cords each in group 1, eight cords each in group 2, and four cords each in group 3.

- Tie a 16-cord half-knot spiral with 103 half knots using group 1 and group 3 cords as the working cords and group 2 cords as the filler cords.

- Put the cords into two groups, each with eight cords.

- Take the first eight-cord group and divide it into three groups that are two cords each, four cords the next, and two cords the third.

- Tie an 8-cord half-knot spiral using 18 half knots, using group 1 and group 3 cords as the working cords and group 2 cords as the filler cords.

- For the second group of eight chords, repeat steps 6 and 7. Your first swing handle is now finished.

- To create a second swing handle, repeat steps 1 through 8 with the remaining eight 16 m (52 1/2 ft.) pieces of rope and the second metal ring, ensuring that the length of the half-knot spiral patterns on each swing handle is the same.

- Place the pine wood seat horizontally and pass a cord through each of the corner holes that have been drilled.

- To anchor the seat in place at each corner, flip the seat over and tie each group of cords with an overhand knot. Make sure the seat is turned up properly and that it is exactly level.

- Fray the cords after cutting them to the proper length.

- The swing is complete and ready to be strung up once the carabiner hooks are attached to the metal rings.

8.8 Geometric Window Valance

The single window opening that this window valance is intended to suit is. To make the piece wider and adequate for a double-window opening, add or remove a section (14 strands). A macramé valance will let in a ton of light while still bringing warmth and style to the decor of your space. For a room with several windows, make extras.

Working time: 12–24 hours (weekend project)

Cords: 4–6mm nylon or polypropylene cord, braided or twisted cotton rope

Supplies:

- (48) 12' (3.66m) 6 mm polypropylene strands (color A)

- (7) 15' (4.57m) 6 mm polypropylene cord strands (color B)

- 20' (6.10m) 6 mm polypropylene cord strands (color B)

- Crochet hook (optional)

- Drapery rod with mounting kit and finials (rod must be capable of expanding to 60" [1.52m])

Directions:

- Using lark's head knots, attach the string to the drapery rod and suspend it there. The 20' (6.10m) strand is attached to one end, and the lark's head knot is offset such that the strands dangle long outside (approximately 7' to 8' [2.13 to 2.44m] inside and the rest 11' to 12' [3.35 to 3.66m] outside). A design of twelve 12' (3.66m) strands and two 15' (4.57m) strand pieces on either side of that portion should be used to hang the remaining cables. At the conclusion, a single 15' (4.57m) strand will be suspended.

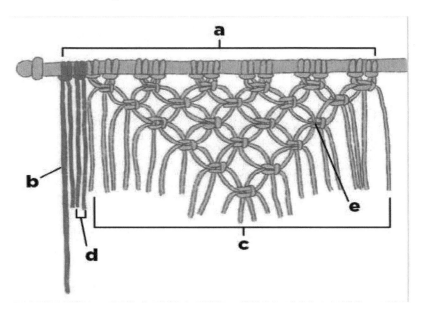

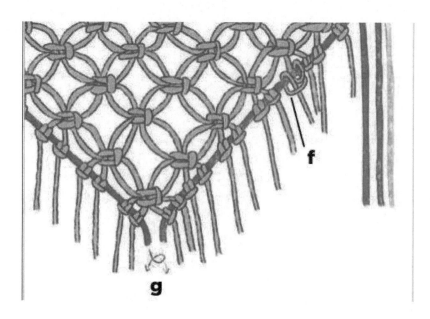

- From the portions of 12' (3.66m) strands, tie a row of square knots. Drop the first two and last two strands on each row to create alternate square knots that will form a descending point. One square knot will be present in the last row.

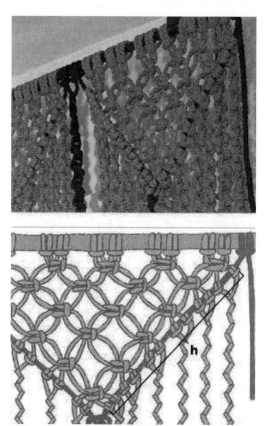

- Draw the contrasting strand next to the opposite strand along the triangle created by the square knots. To make a diagonal edge, connect the dangling strands using a series of cow hitches. At the intersection of the diagonal strands, tie a Josephine knot.

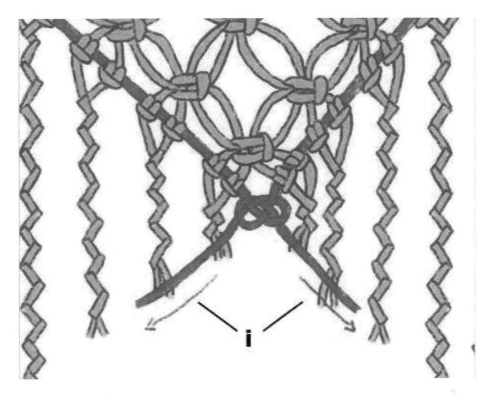

- Create a series of alternating half-hitches by pairing off the strands. Columns contain 3 knots, 7 knots, 13 knots, 17 knots, 23 knots, and 27 knots, working outward from the center.

TIP: On the section's left side, create half-hitches going from right to left. Form half-hitches on the right side of the segment going from left to right. This will make the decreasing angle more obvious.

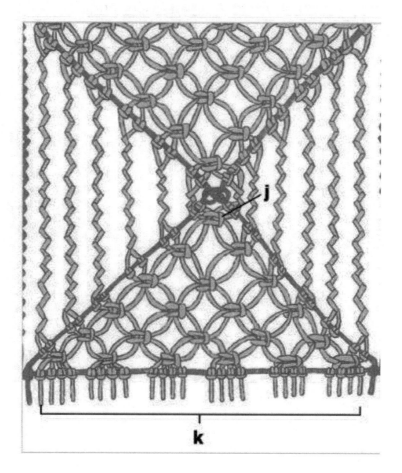

- Double hitch each of the two opposing strands onto the cord as you draw them diagonally away from the center.

- Create a square knot by going back to the section's center. Add two strands for every row, then go on with the alternating pattern until there are six rows.

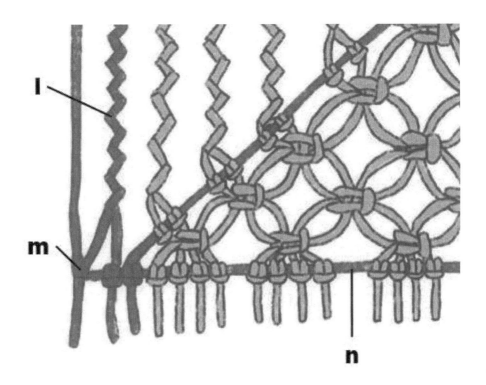

- For each of the next three sections, repeat steps 2 through 6. Alternate half-hitches should be tied to the loose, contrasting strands in between each part until the bottom of the knotted portions is level with the knotted column.

- To make the ends square, tie alternate half-hitches to the two ends. Double-clove hitches are tied to the ends of each cord as you draw the long strand across the bottom of the project. Draw the line back across the bottom at the end of the row, continuing to hitch the cord to the bottom to create a second row. Add an alternate half-hitch to finish.

- Either use a hook to weave the ends into the project's back or trim the ends equally to create a fringe. Install over a window.

8.9 Tassel Reading Nook

The Rullen light fixture from Ikea served as the foundation for this project, but if a light is not wanted, the design can be attached to a Hula-Hoop. Since the hanging tassels are created with just the wrap and square knots, this project is an excellent choice for a beginner. The other components of the project require only the most fundamental crafting abilities, such as grommet hammering, measuring, and light sewing (if desired).

Working time: 4 hours

Cords: Yarns (acrylic or cotton)

Supplies:

- Ceiling hooks (this might accompany the lamp kit)

- 18" (46cm) Rullan light fixture (if the nook is not used with illumination, a metal ring or Hula-Hoop can be used in its place)

- Hanging lamp kit with the light bulb

- Pins (recommended)

- (4–6) worsted-weight skeins of cotton or acrylic yarn

- Hammer (for grommets)

- 5–6 yd. (4.57–5.49m) of sheer, semi-sheer, or lace fabric (at least 50' [1.27m] wide)

- (40) 5 / 32 " (4mm) metal grommets

- Sewing machine or thread and needle (optional)

Directions:

- Cut the cloth into two pieces measuring between 7 1/2" and 8" (2.29 and 2.44m) (cut the bolt fabric in half). Optional: Sew one side of the two panels together. Allow a seam allowance of 1/4" (0.64 cm).

- To keep it stable, fold down the top edge by about 1" (2.54 cm) and secure it with pins. Place the pins along the two panels, with at least 20 being evenly spaced apart.

- By cutting a tiny hole into the cloth about 3/4" (1.91cm) from the folded end, adding a grommet, and hammering it down flat, you can attach grommets (follow the instructions on the package).

- Place the panels aside and make the foundation for the 40 tassels. A piece of yarn should be wrapped around four fingers 20 times or until the desired fullness is reached. With the ends of this hanging strand left untied, add a 12" (30.48cm) piece of matched yarn to the top center and tie it off with a square knot. Do not wrap or trim the tassels at this point.

- Start at the fabric panel's end. Tassels should be threaded through grommets by passing the strands behind the ring, over top of it, and then through a series of two to three square knots to secure them. Repeat around the lamp frame. Each quadrant should have ten tassels tied to it.

- TIP: To enable the curtain to be drawn from side to side, crisscross the tassel ties at the spokes, excluding the final tassel. This will ensure that the curtain's weight is evenly distributed and steady.

- Using yarn in a contrasting color, wrap each tassel. Take pictures of the hanging threads that were used to secure the tassels to the ring. The length of the wrap strands should be around 12" (30.48 cm). Tassel loops should be clipped and trimmed to have even ended. Optional: To stop the wrap from unraveling over time, dab a small amount of clear-drying craft glue onto the cut point on the wrap.

- The lamp kit was fastened to the ring's center before being suspended from the ceiling.

8.10 Comfy Chair

Although this frame is put together using an Ikea Poäng base, it may be customized to fit any chaise. Polypropylene cord is advised for use due to its indoor/outdoor stability and degree of comfort. If the chair is only used indoors, a soft, braided cotton cord filled with dense filler may be utilized in its place.

Working time: 4 hours

Cords: Polypropylene cord

Supplies:

- Ikea Poäng armchair frame

- 512' (156.06m) of 6mm polypropylene cord: cut 16' (40.64cm)–long pieces (32 pieces in total)

- Ikea Poäng lower seat cushion (no back part needed)

- Pliers and sandpaper (optional)

- Safety lighter (for cord melting)

Directions:

- Follow all the directions to assemble the armchair, but skip adding the hook and loop strips.

- TIP: Create the chair's back portion first, then tie the macramé pattern in place. This will make tying the knot simpler. Optional: It will take some effort to remove the staples if you decide to do so. After removing the staple with pliers, sandpaper should be used to finish the job. It is not necessary because this component will be entirely covered.

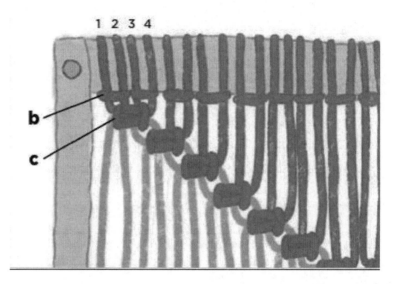

- Create lark's head knots on the top bar by locating the center of each of the 32 cord strands. At the end of this phase, you should have 64 functioning strands after beginning with 32 total strands.

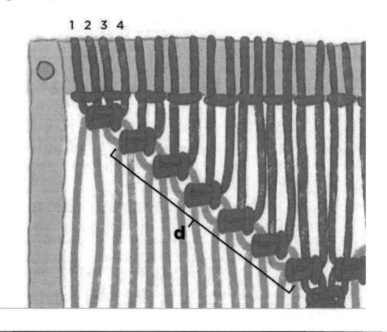

- Create square knots with four strands as indicated. Knots are located from 1 to 4, 29 to 32, 33 to 36, and 61 to 64 working from left to right.

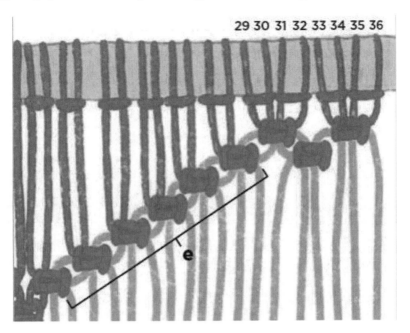

- By adding just two strands to the previous square knot on the following row, create six right-descending alternate square knots beginning from the left. Place the knots evenly so that the last one rests about 1" (2.54cm) from the bar.

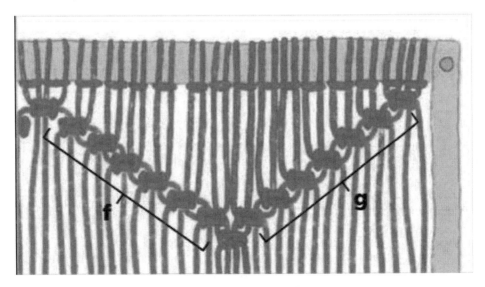

- From the top bar, locate the two center square knots. Create six alternating square knots in the left and right directions, starting with the left knot. Step 4 is repeated in reverse: Make six left-descending alternate square knots starting with the top right square knot. Make sure the knots are level by eyeballing them.

- Connect the top center knots to the two bottom points that are closest to the bar by tying four-strand square knots.

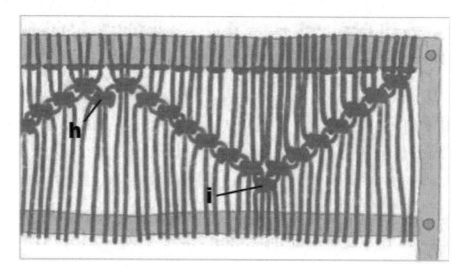

- Each hanging strand should be hacked onto the second bar from left to right, maintaining the string taut and straight throughout.

- As each strand is hitched to the bar, continue to compress the rope to the left. The cord will be firmly placed into this bar.

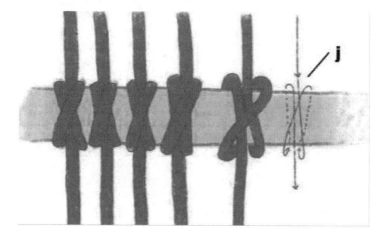

- If a zigzag pattern is preferred, repeat steps 3 through 7 on the following two pieces. Create four-strand square knots from strands 15 to 18 and 46 to 49 to create the diamond shape. To create the diagonal descending square knots, follow the same steps as before, adding two strands. Where the two center diagonal points come together, tie a second square knot.

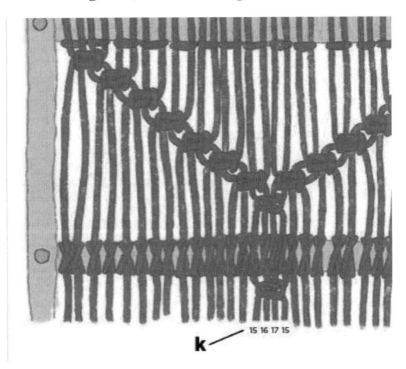

- In the third section, repeat steps 3 through 7.

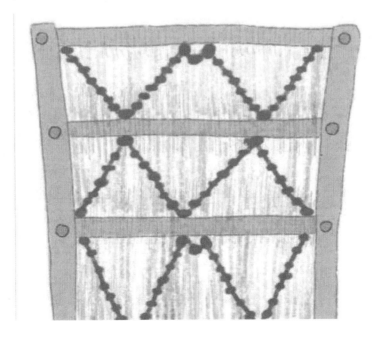

- Finish by gathering eight-strand groupings of the strands below the bottom bar. The first and eighth strands from each group can be used to create two alternate vertical larks' head knots, or you can use these two strands to create a 2" (5.08cm)-long half-knot over the bundle. To the required length, trim and melt the ends using a safety lighter (about 4" [10.16cm]).

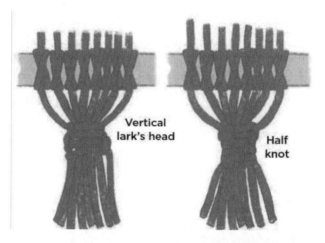

Vertical lark's head

Half knot

- Add the seat cushion after completing the chair's other components.

8.11 Bottle Holder

This beautiful holder would be great for storing a special bottle of wine. It could also be used to show off your favorite glass vase, and it could even be used to hang plants. It has rustic hanging straps that are woven together, and a strong wrapped handle. This piece is made of jute and goes well with a color scheme that is based on natural, earthy colors.

Working time: 2 hours

Supplies:

- Glass jar measuring 26cm (10 1/4 in) high with an 8cm (3 1/8 in) diameter base

- 44.3m (146 1/4 ft.) 2 mm in length (3/32 in) jute

Preparation:

- Cut one 30cm (1ft) 2 mm in length (3/32 in) jute

- Cut sixteen 2.5m (8 1/4 ft.) 2 mm in length (3/32 in) jute

- Cut one 4m (13 1/4 ft.) 2 mm in length (3/32 in) jute

Directions:

- Cut and knot.

- Each string length should be around three yards wide. Cut the four lengths.

- A loop should be made at the knot after they have been folded in half and tied together at the halfway point. Wherever the ceiling or wall is, it is where you would hang the completed project.

- Divide the cords into two pairs, each with two cords. When tying the pairs together, keep in mind to leave approximately four to five inches from the top of the knot.

- Next, tie a spiral knot pattern beneath each set of knots.

- Keep the right chord taut while holding a pair. Through the established loop, pass the left cord over the right, up, and across the back. Firmly pull it.

- Holding the initial right chord taut while you repeat this cycle with the same cord, you should eventually see the beginnings of a spiral knot.

- When the spiral knots are about four inches long, continue making spiral knots.

- Leave around 12 inches of cord length on each set of pairs once you have spirally tied all your pairs. In the middle, at the 12-inch mark, tie a knot for each pair of strings.

- Distribute each pair of them. Take the cord at right from the leftmost set, and tie it to the left chord of the next set down, about three inches below the tie, with the cord at left from the leftmost set. Switch between pairs as you go around the cycle. The final two outer cords should be taken and tied together.

- Tie all the cords together in one large knot about three inches below the range of knots. After around 12 inches, cut the ends of the hanging string.

- In a mason jar, place the plant of your choice and add dirt to it. According to the size of your foliage, it might be best to plant it first, then fit the Mason jar within the macramé hanger.

- Hang and enjoy!

Chapter 9: Wall Hangings

9.1 Layered Birch Hanging

This wall hanging was created to resemble birch wood. Craft stores carry manufactured birch limbs, which are used to make the dowel. To honor nature, substitute discovered branches if at all possible. Use ribbon instead of cloth strips for a less rustic appearance.

Working time: 4–6 hours

Cords: Jute string or twine, fabric strips or ribbon

Supplies:

- (2) 1" x 12' (2.54 x 365.76cm) fabric lengths

- (12) 1" x 5' (2.54 x 152.40cm) fabric (or ribbon) lengths

- (10) 5' (152.40cm) jute lengths (assorted colors)

- 2' (60.96cm) fabric or jute length (for hanging)

- 18" (45.72cm) branch (or a dowel rod)

- (4) 6' (182.88cm) jute lengths (assorted colors)

Directions:

- Tie the 2" (60.96cm) strand of material (or jute) to the branch's ends at both ends.

- Cut tiny holes onto one end of the cloth strips, then tie the 5" (152.4cm)-long strips to the branch using lark's head knots.

- Alternate half-hitches should be used to secure the strands across the row. Drop the first and end strands of the row before beginning the following row. To start forming the net, tie alternate half-hitch knots to each of the strands. The rows of knots should be spaced apart by about 1" (2.54 cm).

- The piece should measure 18" to 20" (45.72 to 50.80 cm) or until there is no more fabric, whichever comes first.

- On either end of the netting, tie the lark's head knots to the 12" (3.66m) pieces of fabric. To each other net opening's center, square knot these strands. The net will become more straight as a result.

- Use overhand knots to join the jute's disjointed hues and then lark's head knots to attach each piece to the branch in between the first two pairs of fabric.

- Create Josephine knots in the fabric netting design, placing each completed knot in the free space.

- Use lark's head knots to tie and install the 6" (182.88cm) strands on either end of the jute net. To aid in straightening the edge of each net opening, tie square knots there.

- If necessary, trim the bottom fringe and hang it.

9.2 Circle Wall Hanging

This substantial wall hanging has multiple uses and doubles as a tiny rug. The piece's unusual shape is achieved with just a few simple knots, and you can alter the rope's color to match your decor. Cotton rope can be replaced with jute if you want to use the piece as a rug.

Working time: 4 hours

Supplies:

- Metal rings: one 29cm (11 3/8 in); one 6cm (2 3/8 in); one 65cm (25 1/2 in); one

55cm (22in)

- 158.4m (527ft) 8 mm in length (5/16 in) rope

Preparation:

- Cut twenty-four 60cm (23 1/2 in) 8 mm in length (5/16 in) rope

- Cut forty-eight 3m (10ft) 8 mm in length (5/16 in) rope

Directions:

- Reverse lark's head knots are used to attach sixteen 3 m (10 ft.) lengths of rope to the 6 cm (2 3 8 in) metal ring such that the mounted rope completely encircles the ring. Placing the ring on a flat surface will cause the cords to extend outward.

- Tie eight square knots around the ring's circumference directly beneath the ring.

- Keeping the ring flat on the work surface & the cords spreading out from the ring, alternate the cords, drop down 4 cm (1 1/2 in), and tie a row of eight square knots.

- Directly below, tie eight more square knots.

- Make sure the 29cm (11 3/8 in) metal ring is evenly spaced all the way around, then set it on top of the cords. As of right now, this will serve as the holding cord.

- Double half hitches should be used to secure the cords to the ring, making sure that each cord group is appropriately separated from the other.

- Use all 32 of the remaining 3m (10ft) lengths of rope to install four 3m (10ft) lengths of rope with reverse lark's head knots in each of the eight gaps to cover the ring between the cord groupings.

- Tie 24 square knots around the ring's circumference directly beneath it.

- One of the square knots tied in step 8 should be placed beneath four other cords. From there, tie six more square knots to form a sinnet of seven square knots with no gaps in between.

- Create a half-knot spiral sinnet using the following four cords, using a total of twelve half knots.

- This design, which alternates square knot and half knot spiral sinnets, can be continued around the ring by repeating steps 9 and 10.

- Make sure the 55cm (22 in) metal ring is evenly separated from the second ring all the way around before placing it on top of the cords. As of right now, this will serve as the holding cord. Ensure the sinnets are uniformly placed around the ring when you double-half hitch the cords to it.

- Using reverse lark's head knots, attach the twenty-four 60cm (23 1/2 in) lengths of rope to the ring, one in each interval between the sinnets.

- Tie 36 square knots around the ring's circumference directly beneath it.

- Place a further row of 36 square knots right below the first row.

- Make sure the 65cm (25 1/2 in) metal ring is evenly separated from the third ring all the way around before placing it on top of the cords. As of right now, this will serve as the holding cord. Double half hitches should be used to secure the cords to the ring.

- Cut the cords to 6 cm (2 3 8 in) length and fray.

9.3 Boho Owl

We choose to revive the popular macramé owl fad from the 1970s with this adorable craft that is ideal for anyone who has extra strands of ribbon or cord laying around. This is a straightforward yet audacious way to deal with craft waste and put it on display for everyone to see.

Working time: 30–60 minutes

Cords: Fabric strips, yarn, ribbon, cotton cord

Supplies:

- (2) 15mm plastic animal eyes with backs

- (12–16) 5' (1.52m) different cord strands

Directions:

- Two bunches of cords should be gathered, and the ends should be tied together with huge overhand knots.

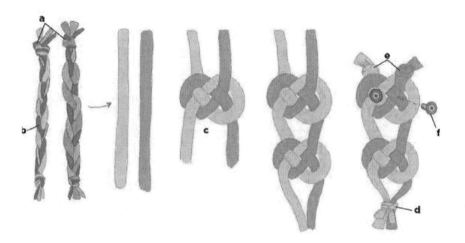

- Divide the groups into three substantial parts, then braid them. Add another sizable overhand knot to the end to secure it.

- Use the two braided sections to tie two sizable Josephine knots.

- Make the overhand knots loose. To tie the cords together, gather them at the bottom and wrap a scrap of cord around it. Fold the free parts in half and tie them off to create the owl horns (for hanging).

- Insert the eyes. In the upper Josephine knot, mount the eyes. If there are no flat pieces to hold the eye posts, wiggle eyes can be used instead and glued to the shape.

9.4 Feathered Hanging

Feather bomb! This straightforward hanging has two layers: the kite tail-like fabric "feathers" on the back layer drip color into the foreground's neutral-toned cotton yarn feathers. This is a great method to utilize leftover fabric scraps, much like the Patch Scrap Mat.

Working time: 2 hours

Cords: Cotton cord, cotton string, fabric strips, or ribbon

Supplies:

- (30) 8" (20.32cm) cotton cord pieces

- (6) 1" x 14"–18" (2.54 x 35.56–45.72cm) fabric (or ribbon) lengths

- 2' (60.96cm) length of 2–3mm cotton cord (for hanging)

- (120) 1" (2.54cm)–wide fabric (or ribbon) strips, cut 5"–7" (12.70–17.78cm) long

- Macramé brush

- 3' (91.44cm) cotton cord pieces

- (48) 6" (15.24cm) cotton cord pieces

- 18" (45.72cm) branch (or a dowel rod)

Directions:

- To hang the branch, tie the 2" (60.96cm) length of jute to both ends of the branch.

- Each of the long fabric strips should have a small hole drilled into one end. Then, tie the lark's heads knots across the branch. Tie a knot in the cloth strips' tips.

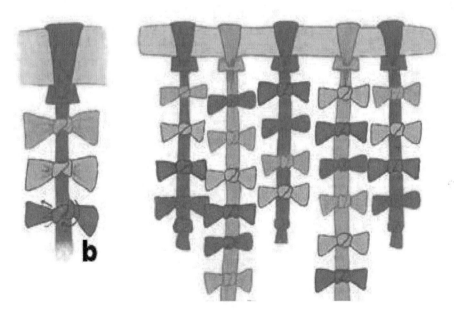

- Half-knots should be used to attach each tiny cloth strip to the long thread to fill the feathers. It should take 15 to 20 strips to fill up each feather. Optional: To add more feathering, make tiny cuts in the fabric.

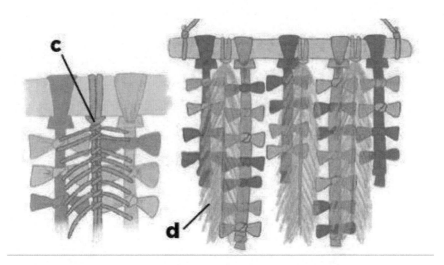

- Fold the 3' (91.44cm) lengths of cord in half to form the front feathers, and then secure them to the branch with lark's head knots. Put the end in an overhand knot. Ten 8" (20.32cm) segments of cotton should be tied with a half-knot to the top of the feather. 16 6" (15.24cm) sections should be tied into the feather's lower half. To give a feather a broader appearance, untangle its twists and fluff.

9.5 Hanging Basket

This multipurpose hanger has a basket-like design, making it suitable for use as a hanging fruit bowl in the kitchen, a craft caddy in your sewing room, or a plant hanger in the conservatory. The basket's enclosure is made of lovely net-like patterns made of alternating square knots.

Working time: 2 hours

Supplies:

- 167m (553ft) 2.5 mm in length (1/8 in) rope

- Two 20cm (7 7/8 in) cane rings

- 6cm (2 3/8 in) metal ring

Preparation:

- Cut forty 4m (13 1/4 ft.) 2.5mm in length (1/8 in) rope

- Cut one 1m (3 1/4 ft.) 2.5mm in length (1/8 in) rope

- Cut three 2m (6 1/2 ft.) 2.5mm in length (1/8 in) rope

Directions:

- A 2m (6 1/2 ft.) length of rope should be wrapped around the 6cm (2 3/8 in) metal ring.

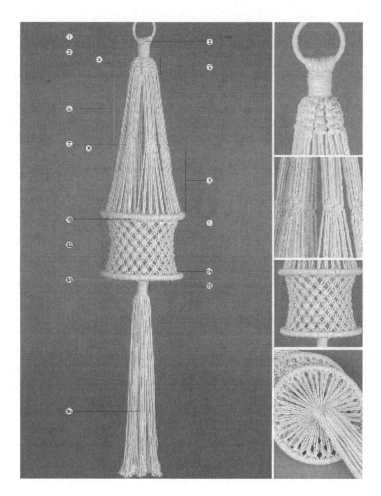

- Fold the forty 4m (13 1/8 ft.) lengths of rope in half over the inside of the ring to mount them.

- Directly beneath the ring, tie all cords together with one of the 2m (6 1/2 ft.) lengths of rope using a 3.5cm (1 3/8 in) wrapped knot.

- Divide the cords into eight sets of ten cords, one under the wrapped knot. Now, every group will be a sinnet. For each sinnet, repeat steps 5-8.

- Use four filler cords and three working cords on each side to tie four 10-cord square knots.

- Four filler cords and one working cord are used on each side to create a 6-cord square knot as you descend 17cm (6 3/4 in).

- Three filler cords and one working cord on each side are used to tie two 5-cord square knots directly beneath.

- Another 6-cord square knot with four filler cords and one working cord on each side is tied below it using the middle six strands.

- All of the cords should be inserted within the first cane ring, which should be lowered 17cm (6 3/4 in). The holding cord will now be attached to the cane ring that is lying horizontally. Triple-half hitches should be tied onto the cane ring with each string.

- Twenty square knots in a row should be tied precisely beneath the initial cane ring to secure it.

- Another row of twenty square knots is tied after lowering 1.5cm (5/8 in) and switching the cords.

- For an additional eight rows, keep repeating the alternate square knot pattern.

- Inside the second cane ring, enclose all cords. The holding cord will now be attached to the cane ring that is lying horizontally. Triple-half hitches should be tied onto the cane ring with each string.

- The rope should be tightly gathered and raised until it is level with the cane ring and in the middle. The hanging basket will have a basis thanks to this. Use the 1m (3 1/4 ft.) piece of rope to secure with a double overhand knot.

- Tie a 3.5cm (1 3/8 in) wrapped knot on top of the double overhand knot using the remaining 2m (6 1/2 ft.) of rope.

- To the desired length, cut the cords.

9.6 Knotty Owls

This owl pattern is pretty easy because you only have to make a few knots. Working with fabric is interesting because it can fray, but if you do not want that shabby-chic look, ribbons will work just as well.

Working time: 2 hours

Cords: Fabric strips, yarn, ribbon

Supplies:

- (2) Plastic eyes (15mm)

- (13) 1" x 36" (2.54 x 91.44cm) fabric pieces

- Optional macramé board with T-pins

- A cotton thread or an oval bead

Directions:

- Tie an overhand knot at the end of a strip of fabric. Then, use clove hitches to attach the other twelve strands to the same strip. Tie a second overhand knot in the first strip, then cut off the extra fabric. Put the rest of the trimming away for now.

- Tie four half-hitches next to each other along the whole row.

- Find the two strips in the middle and thread the bead on them. If you do not have a bead, wrap the strands together with a different color of thread. The length of the wrap should be about 1 inch (2.54 cm).

- **Tip for Cutting Fabric:** Fold the fabric so that it can be cut with fabric shears into ribbons that are 2" (5.08cm) wide. If you tie too many knots in the fabric, it will fray. Use 5/8" to 1" (1.59 to 2.54cm) ribbon instead to avoid the "fray" look.

- Use the first and fifth strands to make a big, loose square knot on each side of the bead. This is meant to look like the eyes of an owl.

- Make a row of two half-hitches next to each other. Drop the first and last strands on the next row and make another row of half-hitches.

- Do step 5 again to make three more rows.

- Cut the remaining piece of scrap fabric in half. Use clove hitches to connect the first 6 strands to the scrap. Pull the knots together, then wrap the fabric around the gathered strands and tie it off with a square knot on the back of the leg. Do the same with the other leg.

- Cut the strings hanging down, which are about 3" (7.62cm) long.

- For each eye, cut three squares from scraps of fabric and cut a hole in the middle. Put the owl's eyes on.

9.7 Kite Tail Curtain

Make these beaded curtains in a boho style. With this project, you can hide a beautiful stash of fabric in plain sight. The size of this curtain is easy to change so that it fits any doorway or window. Double the height of the curtain space to get the length of the cord. The width is equal to the number of strands, which is measured in inches. This project is pretty simple, but it makes a strong point.

Working time: 4 hours

Cords: Heavy yarns, braided or twisted cotton string or twine, fabric strips

Supplies:

- (36) 13" (3.96m) cotton cord strands

- 216 pieces of fabric clippings (about ¼" [0.64cm]–wide strips cut into 8"–10" [20.32–25.40cm] lengths)

- Drapery with a spring-loaded opening that fits a window or door (or substitute with a 3 ½' [1.07m] cotton cord strand with mounting tacks)

- 216' (65.84m) cotton crochet yarn (various colors cut into 12" [30.48cm] lengths)

Directions:

- Use a lark's head knot to tie the 36 strands of cotton cord to the drapery rod. There will be 72 strands that hang down.

- Make one row of square knots, then another row of square knots that change places. This will help keep the curtain in place and spread out the strands that hang down.

- Attach three fabric strips and three pieces of yarn to each length of cord using a square knot. Spread the cotton yarn and fabric pieces out evenly, switching between the yarn and fabric pieces.

- Tie an overhand knot at the end of each strand to keep it from fraying and to make the ends heavier.

- Hang as you like.

9.8 Cotton Candy Dream Catcher

This dream catcher sings for good mornings and beautiful dreams charmingly and dreamily. The ribbons that are used to encircle the ring are quite thick—the thicker, the better! A delectable cocktail for the eyes is created by the combination of textures and volumes. The little color accents sewn into the web represent dreams that have been captured and converted into sugar.

Working time: 8 to 10 hours

Cords: Yarns, cotton string or twine, ribbon, jute string

Supplies:

- 12"–15" (30.48–38.10cm) metal ring
- 30'–36' (9.14–10.97cm) cotton yarn length or 1mm hemp
- About 100 yds. (91.44m) of cotton yarn in assorted (coordinating) colors
- (3) 2 yd. (1.83m) lengths of assorted ribbon
- Tape
- Macramé brush (optional)

Directions:

- One of the three ribbons should be loosely taped to the metal ring. Braid the ring till the ribbon runs out.

- Release the tape once you have returned to the start. Cover the beginning and end by tucking, weaving, and tying the ends.

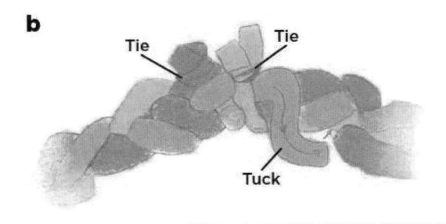

- Make a web on the interior of the metal ring and attach one end of the cotton string to it. To make this process simpler, cut this into 12" to 15" (3.66 to 4.57m) parts. By simply tying the fresh and old ends together with an overhand knot, you can add more cord. Once you have located the center, tie off and cut off the extra material.

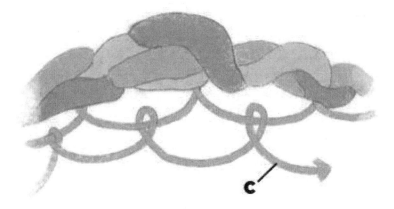

- Cut a length of yarn between 18 and 24 inches (45.72 and 60.96 cm) long, and make a succession of lark's head knots on the cord at the dream catcher's base to create feather-like shapes. At the cord's end, tie an overhand knot.

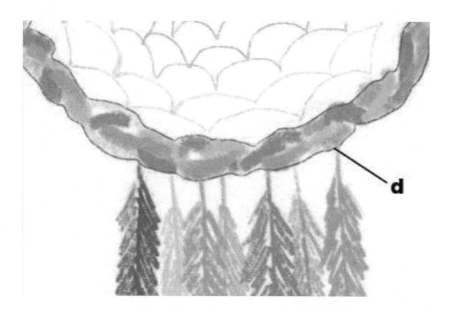

- Cut 40 to 50 pieces of the same rope measuring 12" (30.48 cm) for the smaller feathers and 70 to 80 pieces for the larger feathers. To attach two pieces to the hanging strand, locate the centers of them and tie a reef knot. Continue doing this until the feather reaches the desired level of fullness.

- Brush the feathers to give them a little more puff if desired.

- As many feathers as you like to add, tie tiny cuts from the cord (2" to 3" [5.08 to 7.62cm] pieces) to various places in the webbing to represent caught dreams as an additional embellishment.

9.9 Macramé Mirror Wall Hanging

Start with this easy DIY Bohemian Macramé Mirror Wall Hanging. Only a few knots need to be learned for one fantastic creation.

Working time: 1 hour

Supplies:

- Wood Ring: 2 inch

- Macramé Cording: 4mm

- Octagon Mirror

- Sharp Scissors

- Wood Beads: 25mm w/10mm Hole Size

Directions:

- Section off 4 pieces of macramé cording into 108-inch (3-yard) lengths.

- Use a Lark's Head knot to secure all four of the folded strips to the wood loop. Tighten and cinch the knots together. Split two Lark's Head knots, then begin to tie them together into a square knot.

- Knot two squares together.

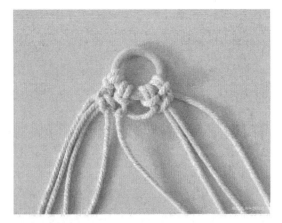

- To the second pair of Lark's Head knots, begin tying two square knots.

- To create a single, broad square knot, unite the two square knots as you begin the second one by looping one of their sides through it.

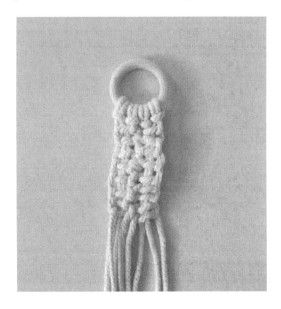

- 7 square knots total should be tied down on both sides.

- After making the knots, cut the ends off. Four strings in the middle, two on each side. To repair the frayed ends of the cording, tape the ends. The beads can then be added more easily as a result. Congrats! The difficult thing was that! The last steps consist of making simple knots and leveling the sides.

- To each of the two side cording lines, add one bead. Make an equal knot on both sides under the bead. Place a plain or (Overhand) knot on the four cords in the center, about 1/14 inch below the beads.

- Add one of the middle cords to the other two on the sides. Put a knot in all three at the top and bottom. To make the knot lengths uniform, add the mirror. To keep the mirror in place, attach one of the three side cords to the rear.

- All three side cords at the bottom left, and right of the mirror should be tied in basic knots. Re-separate the cords on the three sides. Send one from each side to the mirror's rear, then bring two from each side to the front and bind them together.

- Bind all the strings together before flipping the mirror over. Reverse the mirror, then cinch the front knot. Hold the knot after slipping the rear strings inside. Reduce the cord's end to a length of about 14 inches. Pull the rope's ends apart. Use a comb to comb the cord's ends to the edges of the fluff.

9.10 Giant Dreams

This beautiful dream catcher was made with colors that make you think of dreams and fabric that flows. We liked the idea of putting an embroidery hoop into the design, and when it was paired with some pretty lace, it gave it the perfect vintage look. Since a Hula Hoop is used to make the outside ring, this huge dream catcher will be easy to hang.

Working time: 3–6 hours

Cords: Mixed cord, cotton yarn, ribbon, jute rope, cotton rope, twine, burlap

Supplies:

- 24" (60.96cm) Hula-Hoop

- Ribbon of mixed colors and textures (4" [10.16cm] burlap ribbon, assorted lacy ribbons, cotton thread, and sheer satin ribbons)

- 12" (30.48cm) embroidery hoop

- 12' (3.66m) a neutral-colored strand of cotton yarn

- 14" x 14" (35.56 x 35.56cm) a lace piece or a big doily

- Large-eye needle (optional)

- 15' (4.57m) length of 4" (10.16cm) burlap ribbon

- Transparent craft glue (optional)

Directions:

- Take the Hula-Hoop to its most basic parts. Tape one end of the burlap ribbon to the Hula-Hoop and start wrapping it around. If you need to, glue the ends of the wrapped burlap together to keep it stable.

- Tie the ends of 2 colorful ribbons together in the middle of the underside of the Hula-Hoop with an overhand knot. Make loose half-knots around the Hula-Hoop, about 1 1/2 inches (3.81 cm) apart, to cover it. Once you are back at the beginning, weave the ends into the circle quietly.

- Attach a piece of lace fabric or a doily to an embroidery hoop. If you need to, add a little glue to keep the fabric in place on the back. Cut away any extra fabric.

- Tie the Hula-Hoop to one end of the 6" (182.88cm) piece of cotton yarn. Thread it through a hole in the edge of the mounted lace, and then loop the yarn back to the Hula-Hoop. Keep threading the embroidery hoop onto the Hula-Hoop, ensuring the small hoop stays in the middle the whole time. When you get back to the beginning, tie the yarn off and cut off any extra.

- TIP: Put a piece of tape on the end of the cotton string so that you can use it to thread the doily through the Hula-Hoop. It will look kind of like a needle.

- Tie an extra ribbon to the bottom of the Hula-Hoop to decorate the dream catcher. Braid a few pieces together to add weight and texture to the look. Use fake feathers to make something more interesting. Some ribbons' ends can be cut with slits so that they can be tied to the dream catcher with a lark's head knot.

Chapter 10: Accessories

10.1 Hoop Earrings

This project is a great place to start if you want to learn how to make macramé jewelry. A pair of hoop earrings bought in a store is decorated with round metal beads and a simple square knot pattern. They are so easy to make that you will want to make more than one pair in different colors to match your wardrobe.

Working time: 4 hours

Cords: Heavy yarns, braided or twisted cotton string or twine, fabric strips

Supplies:

- 2.6m (9ft) length of 1mm (1/32 in) your choice of color nylon bead cord

- Six 4mm (5/32 in) metallic circular beads with a 2mm (3/32 in) hole

- Pair of 4cm (1 1/2 in) hoop earrings

Preparation:

- Cut two 1.3m (4 1/2 ft.) 1 mm lengths (1/32 in) nylon bead cord

Directions:

- Fold in half one of the 1.3m (4 1/2 ft.) pieces of nylon bead cord and place it on the inside of one of the hoops.

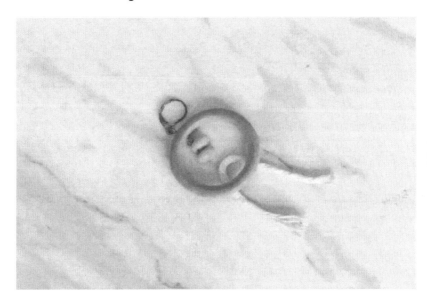

- Use T-pins to hold the hoop earring to a project board. Your filler cord will be the hoop, and the two sides of the folded cord will be your working cords.

- Make a strong square knot as close as you can to where the connector goes into the hoop.

- Make a net with 15 square knots by going around the hoop (your filler cord). Once the sinnet is done, push the knots together hard.

- Thread a metal bead onto the earring hoop and press it firmly against the square knot sinnet.

- Three square knots should be tied right under the bead.

- Repeat step 5.

- Repeat step 6.

- Repeat step 5.

- Just below the bead, tie a chain of sixteen square knots that end right before the connector.

- Use both cords to make a tight double overhand knot.

- Cut the cords to size and carefully burn the ends to keep them from fraying. Use a flame to melt the ends of the cord, but do not let them get too black.

- Repeat steps 1 through 12 for the second hoop earring to make a pair.

10.2 Shopping Bag

This vivid, striking shopping bag may be made with a few straightforward knots. It is the ideal accessory to bring along when you go shopping or are out and about conducting errands. To style your distinctive carrier, you can be creative with the handles you select, but keep in mind that they must match the designated cords.

Working time: 4 hours

Cords: Heavy yarns, braided or twisted cotton string or twine, fabric strips

Supplies:

- 60cm (23 1/2 in) 5 mm in length (1/4 in) rope in a color of your preference

- Three 32m (106ft) 5 mm in length (1/4 in) ropes in colors of your preference

- Two hardwood bag handles of your choosing, with inner widths no narrower than 12.5 cm (4 7/8 in)

Preparation:

- Cut eight 4m (13 1/4 ft.) lengths from each of the 32m lengths of 5mm (1/4 in) rope in the various colors, giving you a total of twenty-four 4m (13 1/4 feet) lengths

Directions:

- Take your first bag handle, and using a reverse lark's head knot, attach twelve 4 m (13 1/4 ft.) lengths of rope to it, alternating the colors as you go. The mounted rope should have a width of 12.5cm (4 78 in). This will be the first handle.

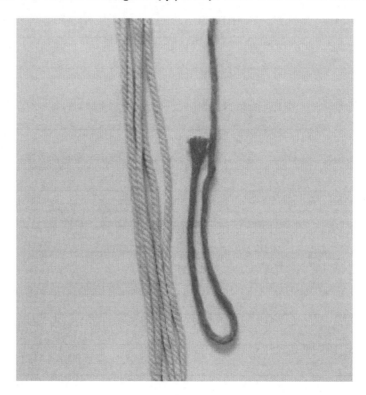

- The remaining twelve 4m (13 1/4 ft.) pieces of rope should be mounted using the second bag handle, as indicated in step 1. The second handle will be this.

- Tie a row of six extremely tight square knots right beneath the handle, beginning with handle 1.

- Dropdown 1.5cm (5/8 in), alternate the cords and tie a row of five square knots.

- Alternate the cords, then make a series of six square knots at a distance of 2 cm (3 in).

- Two more rows with 2cm (3/4 in) intervals in between should be tied in an alternate square knot design.

- Make sure the knotted region on handles 1 and 2 is the same length by repeating steps 3-6 on handle 2.

- Number the cords from 1 to 24 for handle 1.

- The cords for handle 2 are numbered 25 to 48.

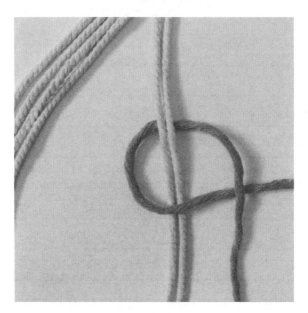

- The front of the design should be facing out on both sides of the bag when you bring the handles together. Using cords 48 and 1 as the filling cords and cords 47 and 2 as the working cords, combine cords 1 and 2 with cords 47 and 48 to tie a square knot 4 cm (1 1/2 in) down from the top of the bag.

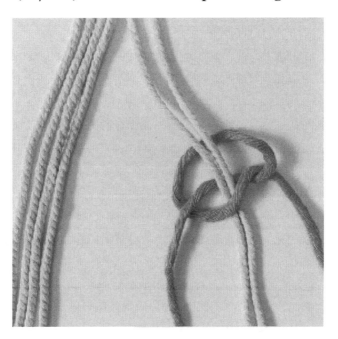

- Similarly, 4cm (1 1/2 in) down, join cords 23 and 24 with cords 25 and 26 to form a square knot, with cords 24 and 25 acting as the working cords and cords 23 and 26 as the filler cords.

- Continue tying five more square knots on each side of the bag to make a row of twelve square knots around it, aligning them with the two square knots tied in stages 10 and 11.

- For another five rows, wrap the bag in an alternate square knot pattern, leaving 4 cm (1 1/2 in) between each row.

- At this point, stitch the bag's bottom edge together. Lay the bag flat, line up the handles equally, and check that the bottom row's twelve square knots are arranged in a straight line, side by side, starting with a knot from the bag's back, moving to the front, and repeating this pattern down the row.

- Place the 60 cm (23 1/2 in) piece of rope exactly below the row of twelve square knots. You can use this as a holding cord.

- Double-half hooks each cord onto the holding cord, working from left to right, ensuring that each cord stays in the order established in step 14.

- Each end of the holding cord should be tied in a tight overhand knot before letting the ends hang down with the working cables. The cords should be pushed tightly together over the holding cord.

- If desired, fray all cords at 5 cm (2 in) after trimming.

10.3 Serenity Bracelet

One of the most common knots in micro macramé can be practiced a lot with this beginner's bracelet. Additionally, you will develop your beading and tension-balancing skills. The finished length of this bracelet, which has a button fastening, is 7 inches.

Working time: 3 hours

Supplies:

- 36 purple seed beads, size 11
- White C-Lon cord, 6 ½ ft., x 3
- 18 frosted purple size 6 beads
- 1 to 5 mm. purple button closure bead (the button bead needs to be able to fit onto all 6 cords)
- 11 cm. purple and white focal bead
- 26 dark purple size 6 beads

Directions:

- Fold each of the three cords in half. Locate the center, then set it up on your work surface.
- Now, while holding the cords, loosely tie an overhand knot in the middle.
- The buttonhole closure will now be created. Take each outer cord and tie a flat knot just below the knot (aka square knot). Flat knots should be tied until you have around 2 1/2 cm.
- Make a horseshoe shape with the ends after untying your overhand knot.
- All six ropes are now gathered together. Consider the cords as being numbered from left to right, 1 through 6. 2 to 5 cords will remain in the center as filler cords.

Use cords 1 and 6 to tie flat knots around the filler cables. (Note: To guarantee a good fit, you can now pass your button bead through the opening. If more or fewer flat knots are required to get a snug fit, do so. A 5 mm bead should fit well in this size. Tie flat knots continuously until you have 4 cm worth. (To lengthen the bracelet, increase the number of flat knots here and in step 10 by an equal number.)

- Set cords 1, 4, and 1 apart. Find the two cords in the middle. Then, using cords 2 and 5.7, create a flat knot. Finally, thread a size 6 purple frosted bead onto them. Cords 1 and 6 will now be used for our work. A seed bead, two size 6 dark purple beads, and a third seed bead are strung on chain 1. Repeat with cord 6, then divide it into cords 3 and 3. Use the remaining 3 cords to tie a flat knot. Use the appropriate 3 cords to tie a flat knot.

- Steps 4 and 5 should be done three times.

- Locate the center 2 cords, clasped together, and the focal bead, measuring 1 cm. Remove the following cords (2 and 5), then bead them as follows: One frosted purple bead, two dark purple beads, and six dark purple beads are used. To bead, locate cords 1 and 6 and do as follows: Two seed beads, one dark purple bead, one seed bead, and two frosted purple beads are strung together.

- Tie a flat knot with cords 2 and 5 around the two middle cords.

- With the help of cords 1 and 6, join the center four cords together and create a flat knot around them.

- Repeat steps 4 and 5 for 4 times.

- Repeat step 3.

- Place your button bead on each of the six cords and secure it with an overhand knot.

10.4 Choker Necklace

This stunning choker-style necklace is made out of delicate square knots that are decorated with metallic beads. The finished item is fastened around your neck by plaited ties. To adjust the necklace longer or shorter to fit, simply change the length of the plaits. Just knot fewer "links" to create a bracelet or anklet that matches your choker necklace.

Working time: 4 hours

Supplies:

- Fourteen 4mm (5/32 in) round metallic beads with 2mm (3/32 in) hole

- 8mm (5/16 in) jump ring

- 12m (40ft) length of 1mm (1/32 in) nylon bead cord of your preference in color

Preparation:

- Cut eight 1mm (1 3/2 in) nylon bead cord lengths of 150cm (5 ft.) each.

Directions:

- Using a T-pin, fasten the jump ring to the top of a project board.

- With reverse lark's head knots, attach four 150 cm (5 ft.) pieces of nylon bead cord to the jump ring.

- Divide the cords into two groups of four cords each, and with each group, tie a sonnet made up of three square knots.

- Number the ropes from 1 to 8. For a metal bead to rest directly on the square knots above it, thread it into cords 4 and 5.

- Use cords 3 and 6 as working cords and cords 4 and 5 as filler cords to tie a square knot directly beneath the metal bead.

- Divide the cords into two groups of four cords each, and with each group, tie a sinnet made up of four square knots.

- Number the ropes from 1 to 8. A metal bead should sit directly up against the square knots above it when it is strung onto cords 4 and 5.

- Use cords 4 and 5 as filler cords and cords 3 and 6 as working cords to tie a square knot directly beneath the metal bead.

- Follow steps 6 through 8 four more times.

- Number the ropes from 1 to 8. Use cords 3-6 as filler cords and cords 1, 2, 7, and 8 as working cords to tie an eight-cord square knot.

- Make an overhand knot with all eight cords directly beneath the eight-cord square knot, and pull it tight to secure it.

- Just below the overhand knot, trim five of the cords, singe the ends to melt them while being careful not to burn them, and then press the melted ends onto the knot.

- Make a 12cm (4 3/4 in) plait with the last three cords, and then secure it with a tight overhand knot.

- Trim the cords to the length you desire after stringing a metal bead onto them and tying a tight overhand knot to keep it in place.

- Reattach the jump ring to the top of the project board after unpinning the partially finished necklace and turning it 180 degrees (the completed half of the choker is still right side facing up, but it is now trailing off of the top of the project board).

- To finish the necklace, carry out steps 2 through 14 on the opposite side of the jump ring.

10.5 Basic Tassel Keychain

Working time: 2 hours

Supplies:

- Off-white or white yarn

- 2 to 4 wooden beads

- 1 key ring

- Your choice of color for the yarn or embroidery floss

- A pair of scissors

Directions:

- Start by tying a 20-inch-long piece of yarn to the key ring with a lark's head knot, also known as a cow hitch knot.

- The wooden beads should be threaded to both ends.

- You should cut nearly 20 pieces of yarn, each of which should be twice as long as the desired length of the tassel. Hold them in an orderly bundle and place them in the middle of the two yarn pieces that are attached to the key ring.

- Make a basic knot using the two yarn pieces and the group of yarns.

- Make sure the beads are all tightly strung and that the tassel is divided into two roughly equal lengths. To fasten, undo the knot, and then proceed to tie another one.

- The tassel's ends should be smoothed together after being folded.

- The neck of the tassel is made using threaded embroidery yarn.

- Pull the loose end around, under, and then around the tassel where you want the top of the neck to start, with the full skein to the right. It is folded up and down to form a loop.

- Using the skein end, wrap the thread around the tassel in a straight line while advancing through the ends. Wrap it back up toward the loop once your neck reaches the proper length.

- Trim the ends and pass them through the loop you just made.

- Pull in the opposite directions with the bottom and top.

- Pull it firmly until the loop disappears into the new neck.

- Trim the ends of the embroidery thread.

- To finish, trim the tassel's ends for a uniform appearance.

10.6 Net Produce Bag

These are ideal for a weekend excursion to the lake, the beach, or the farmer's market. They contain whatever you need, but little crumbs could escape. Especially ideal for trips to the park and the beach.

The good news is that there are only two things needed to make it.

Working time: 2 hours

Supplies:

- Macramé cords

- A pair of scissors

Directions:

- Make sure that the cord is divided into 18 equal strands, each measuring 96 inches. You will also need to cut the main cord, which will knot all the other cords together to a length of about 80 inches. The rope should be folded in half before being looped over the mainline.

- Continue pulling it tightly as you move down the line. To prevent the holes on the bag from being too large, you would want them to be close together, within a half-inch. Along the mainline, advance by roughly 20 inches.

- Once you have completed the entire line or reached the bottom, you will begin to gather one piece from each knot and attach it to the second layer of knots while simultaneously leaving one thread free.

- The other side should be tied in a similar manner. To the bottom and the full length of the bag, you will tie knots.

- Take the additional strand that was left out in step 2 and fold the strand in half.

- The remaining strings will then be threaded through the other two sides as you tie knots between each of the loops to join them together.

- Take another piece of cord and tie a knot at the bottom of the fringe in the front and the back while also trimming the bottom of the fringe.

- Make a knot at the bottom of a second excess cord from the mainline to use as a shoulder strap.

10.7 Clutch Purse

It is easy to amaze your pals on a night out with a handmade macramé clutch purse, and it is the perfect size to hold your party necessities. It is a necessary piece of fashion jewelry because of its attractive chevron flap and magnetic button closing.

Working time: 4 to 5 hours

Supplies:

- 54m (180ft) 3 mm in length (1/8 in) jute

- Hot glue gun

- Three 18mm (1 1/16 in) magnetic snap fasteners

- 56m (186 1/2 ft.) 3 mm in length (1/8 in) rope

Preparation:

- Cut eighteen 3m (10ft.) 3 mm lengths (1/8 in) jute

- Cut eighteen 3m (10ft.) 3 mm lengths (1/8 in) rope

- Cut one 2m (6 1/2 ft.) 3 mm lengths (1/8 in) rope

Directions:

- Using T-pins, fasten the 2 m (6 1/2 ft.) length of rope to a project board, making sure it is solid and straight. You can use this as a holding cord.

- Mount the 18 lengths of jute and 18 lengths of rope, each measuring 3 meters (10 ft.), alternately onto the holding cord using reverse lark's head knots. The installed cords should be centered on the holding cord and have a width of 24.5cm (9 34 in).

- Tie 18 square knots in a row directly beneath the holding cord.

- Tie a row of seventeen square knots using alternating cords.

- For an additional forty-five rows, alternate square knot patterns with no spaces in between the rows, finishing with a row of eighteen square knots. The macramé must be 27cm (10 5/8 in) long overall; if necessary, add additional rows of square knots to make the macramé longer, but keep in mind that it is crucial to finish with a row of 18 square knots.

- Group the cords into three equal groups of twenty-four each: group 1 for the first 1-24 cords, group 2 for the next 25-48 cords, and group 3 for the last 49-72 cords. To make the front flap chevron edge for the finished bag, complete steps 7 through 15 on each of the three sets of cords.

- Work a decreasing square knot pattern on each of the three sets of cords, starting with six square knots and ending with one in the last row, exactly beneath the last row knotted.

- The cords in each of the three groupings are numbered from 1 to 24.

- Make cord 1 a holding cord, bring it diagonally from left to right along the pattern's edge to sit below the single square knot, then tie cords 2–12 together in diagonal double half hitches.

- Create cord 24 as a holding cord, and bring it diagonally from right to left along the pattern's edge to sit precisely beneath the single square knot, then tie cords 13 to 23 together in diagonal double half hitches.

- Cords 1 and 24 on the holding cords should be crossed over to change their positions.

- Now, renumber each group's chords from 1 to 24.

- Make cord 1 a holding cord, move it from left to right, so it is just below the row of diagonal double half hitches, and knot cords 2 through 12 into diagonal double half hitches.

- Making cord 24 a holding cord, tie diagonal double half hitches with cords 13–23 such that they are precisely beneath the row of diagonal double half hitches.

- Double overhand knot linking cords 1 and 24 together.

- The macramé should be taken off the project board. To hide the cords around the chevron edge, turn the macramé over and employ the weaving finish technique. The retaining cord should not be cut at the straight edge.

- Use a hot glue gun to bind the cords in each group by trimming them to a length of 5mm (1/4 in).

- Keep the macramé on the wrong side up, but turn it so that the chevrons are at the top and the straight edge is at the bottom to create a clutch bag. To form the pocket of the bag, fold the bottom border up by 12cm (4 3/4 in).

- Lace-up the edges of the bag pocket using the holding cord, concluding with the cord inside the purse, and tie a double overhand knot to fasten.

- To finish the bag, attach the magnetic snap fasteners. To ensure that they line up when the flap is closed, use a hot glue gun to attach one part of each to the back side of the chevrons and the corresponding part to the front of the bag pocket.

Conclusion

Depending on the ability level, macramé is a very interesting type of art that is simple to master but can be applied in a variety of ways. Simple bracelets to intricate wall hangings can be made by combining knots, loops, and even braiding. You can create so many different things with just this one craft. It is incredible.

To master macramé, one must practice a lot and have patience. Nevertheless, learning is worthwhile because it has so many advantages. The difficulty of macramé appeals to many people.

Macramé has a wide range of applications, making it incredibly versatile. The majority of macramé's works are used for decoration, but some people also utilize it as a way to unwind and decompress. Macramé is a pastime for certain people. Whatever way you choose to use macramé, it will be profitable and satisfying.

The craft is also friendly to the environment. While handcrafted macramé is the most common style, this alternative enables you to create without harming the environment or yourself.

Another craft that may be performed in a tiny area is macramé. It is an excellent project to do when you have few resources because it does not need a lot of room or bulky materials to make.

We hope it was interesting for you to learn more about macramé for beginners and that you will take the time to give it a try. Once you get the hang of it, macramé is a fantastic hobby or way to unwind, and you will be eager to keep making new items.

Printed in Great Britain
by Amazon